# IGNITE YOUR
# PRACTICE WITH
# THE T VISA

*Alexandra Lozano*

*And*

*Helen Tarokic*

# Contents

———✍———

# DEDICATION

Alexandra dedicates this book to Dorothy Johnson, Nana. You survived more than anyone ever should and loved more than anyone ever could. May your soul find the peace that you were never afforded during your life.

Helen dedicates this book to her Amigas, who have taught her more about survival, community and support than she ever dreamed possible, and to her family, who make her laugh every day. A special thank you to Alexandra Lozano, whose support and drive made this book possible.

# PREFACE

As you read this book, you may realize you have overlooked some critical immigration options for your clients. I want you to know that you are not alone. There is still time to contact people and invite them for a new consultation to review a new option you have studied. By reading this book and implementing "T screening" now, you will be ahead of many of your colleagues. It's okay to contact people and be excited and say you may have found something new to talk to them about.

I have taught T visas to lawyers throughout the United States. Attorneys who are experts in humanitarian relief are having that "aha!" moment as I explain that human trafficking is apparently *a very ordinary* experience among many of our clients. Surviving trafficking is so ordinary and horrible that clients don't think to mention it to us. I think deep down, I always knew that many people who came to me for relief - even business immigration clients - had suffered a lot. I thought that asking about their journey or problems with employment didn't make sense because it would not help them get a visa. I was wrong. I thought that trafficking survivors didn't seek our services, and that's why we didn't have T visa cases coming in the door. I was wrong. We would get an occasional referral from a non-profit agency for someone who had escaped sexual or labor-based slavery, and I would do a T visa, but I was only doing T visas when it was obvious that the person qualified. I would avoid CLE classes on T visas because we "did not get T visa cases" – but the truth was, those cases were right under my nose. I did not realize that trafficking survivors were coming into our office and failing to self-identify as victims of human trafficking. To be honest, I wish the word "trafficking" were not a part of the dialogue, because it makes us think only of the scenarios in Hollywood sex trafficking and kidnapping movies. If we instead called it a visa for "economic and sex abuses that may have gone unreported" we would get a lot more interest in the T visa.

I now know to ask about unpaid wages, failure to pay overtime, domestic violence cycles where the abuser has economic control, religious abuses (church control), student and J-1/H-1/H-2A visa abuses, and other scenarios that may trigger a T visa. I know now that I must screen, and re-screen, every potential client for labor and sex abuses, if I want to be sure we have not missed a wonderful option for legalization and a path to permanent residency. Since I have figured this out, I decided to share it with my colleagues. Since the time we began having T visa seminars and brainstorming sessions, I have realized that something very fundamental had been missing from my humanitarian law practice. I had been missing out, and now that I am aware of T visa options, I don't want any of my fellow immigration and employment law attorneys to miss out on these visa options that can save lives. I should also mention that movements to stop trafficking have been growing nationwide. I've been surprised at the support from laymen and women in the community who seem to be attuned to this issue. You may be pleasantly surprised to find human trafficking task forces and community groups to join where you can help others or receive referrals to handle the immigration aspect of a trafficking case.

I am a Board-Certified Immigration Law Specialist in North Carolina. I graduated from Wake Forest University School of Law in 2006. My law office, based in the town of Wilmington, North Carolina, handles business immigration cases, family-based immigration, and humanitarian cases (including Us, Ts and VAWA).

I remember strongly a consultation I did long ago, where the J-2 spouse had written a long story about all the abuse she suffered at the hands of her J-1 husband from whom she had recently separated. At the time, I thought, there is nothing I can do for her since she had fallen out of status. I remember thinking I had a limited time in the consultation, and that I didn't have time to read her sprawling handwritten story, which she tried to give me that day. After all, what would it matter if I read it? She didn't have an alternative sponsor. Looking back, I realize her J-1 spouse had total economic control of her. She lived in fear of her J-1 teacher spouse – and he held her derivative J-2 status over her head while he forced her to have sex whenever he wanted. He treated her like his servant, and his reasoning for that was that she was his woman – she was merely "an African wife who needed to obey her husband." At the time, I thought I was dealing with a domestic violence victim – but I now realize that she was also a survivor of human trafficking and could have applied for a T visa. I don't work at that firm anymore and this was many years ago, but this story stays in my mind. I can still remember what she looked like, and how hopeless she felt. I can only hope that maybe one day she will hear about the T visa from a lawyer who is more knowledgeable about T visas. Maybe later she reported the violence and got a U visa. Maybe she is no longer with us. My opportunity to help her slipped through my hands because my mind was not focused on the concept of human trafficking, and I had not been trained to identify T visa options. Unfortunately, I had never even heard of trauma-informed legal representation at the time.

As immigration lawyers, we generally want to help immigrants. We worry about how they may suffer labor, sex, or domestic abuses when they are undocumented. But have we realized that the anti-trafficking laws and T visa statutes are there to protect these individuals from these abuses and to help them legalize their status? I hope this book sparks a conversation in every law firm.

I hope you begin to identify trafficking situations with ease. I want you to ignite your law practice with new T visa options for your clients. I want you to help survivors of trafficking realize that they are not alone and can legalize their status. I want you to ask the right questions in your consultations so that you identify survivors of trafficking who can't self-identify as victims. I want those survivors to learn to help identify and assist other survivors. I want to stop human trafficking. I hope that every city in America ends up having at least one lawyer who becomes a T visa expert. There are 5000 T visas available every year, and the T visa cap has never been met. We have work to do. If you obtain a T visa for someone, share your victory with me. Each win is exciting and rewarding.

Helen L. Tarokic

# PREFACE

I consider myself a passionate advocate for my clients. I serve the Mexican community almost exclusively. I always try to look for creative solutions and think outside the box to find them some form of immigration relief. Yet despite my best efforts, I was telling more than 50% of my consultations that I did not see any relief for them.

And then I learned about the T Visa.

Like you, I knew about the T Visa in the sex-trafficking context. I figured that the T Visa was something for non-profits where women were rescued and then brought in for services. I thought it had no application to my Mexican, mostly male, clients. I was wrong.

Fortunately for me and my clients, I met Helen. Helen taught me about human smuggling turned human trafficking. Almost every single one of my clients had entered the United States with a "coyote", or human smuggler. What I quickly found out is that the vast majority of my clients had been trafficked to the United States. They were held against their will in the United States by their smugglers (who turned out to be traffickers), forced to work under the threat of death, and either escaped or were ultimately released.

I was floored when I realized this. Now I had a tool that could serve so many people. I could change lives family-by-family with the T Visa. And I have.

As joyful as I am to have this incredible, life-changing relief available to help my clients, I can't help but feel some shame, disappointment, and embarrassment for telling hundreds of that they did not qualify for anything when I simply did not know how the T Visa worked. Now I am committed to teaching others how to use the T Visa with the hopes that no one else makes the mistakes that I did.

Doing great work and earning a great living go hand-in-hand. The T Visa has not just changed the lives of my clients, it has completely transformed my practice. Because so many people qualify for the T Visa, I have been able to take my earnings to the next level. If you know my work through AllyLozano.com or AMIGA Lawyers, you know that I teach that you must charge your worth in cases. I charge my full fee for T Visa cases and do not treat them as pro bono or low bono.

T Visa cases are extremely labor intensive, especially with the recent increase of Requests for Evidence. I urge you to consider this when you are adding T Visas to your practice and ensure that you charge appropriately. It will be worth every cent to your clients.

It is my sincerest hope that this book is the catalyst to igniting your practice with the T Visa and transforming the lives of your clients.

Alexandra Lozano, Es q.

# INTRODUCTION

---◆---

People throughout the world migrate to the U.S. for different purposes. While tourism, sightseeing, sports, and other social activities are among the reasons people come to the United States, the most common reason for seeking to immigrate to the US, whether lawfully or unlawfully, is economic.

However, there are many people who find themselves in the United States forced into situations against their will. For example, upon arriving in the US, an immigrant realizes that her job is going to be different from what she had been promised by her 'agent' who helped her obtain a work visa. The living conditions are inhumane, the work hours are far beyond what was advertised, and she is not paid for overtime, or maybe she is not paid at all.

This is human trafficking.

Human trafficking is the modern reincarnate of the slave industry. The news is rife with the case of those who have been enticed by friends, acquaintances, and relatives into following to the "promised land" in search of a greener pasture only to discover that they've been trafficked.

Another very common situation in which human trafficking occurs starts out with what looks like human smuggling. There are a lot of human smuggling related statutes, all of which are related to borders or checkpoints. For example, 8 USC § 1324(a)(1)(A)(i) makes it an offense to knowingly bring or attempt to bring into the United States an alien at any place other than an official point of entry to the country, such as a port, airport, or land immigration checkpoint. A smuggling crime, for example, happens in the book *The Handmaid's Tale*, when people try to smuggle handmaids out of Gilead and into freedom; and it happens in the real world, along the US-Mexico border when people try to come in without a visa and without being detected. However, human smuggling can quickly turn into human trafficking, which is a crime against a person (i.e. not a border rule). The victim agrees to be brought, or smuggled, into the US unlawfully, and while she is aware of and in agreement with the arrangement, she remains at the mercy of the person that facilitated her travel to the US. She knows that she's an undocumented immigrant whose movements and opportunities to find a job are severely restricted, and until she is released to her family, she is under the complete control of her smuggler.

Once she is brought into the United States, she is then held by the traffickers, who she believed were smugglers, against her will. She is forced to cook, clean, and serve her traffickers – and it is the forced, unpaid labor that is a hallmark of labor trafficking. She is forced to give in to their every demand, which can include performing sex acts for her traffickers or being forced to have sex for money. These victims are completely helpless. The search for an economic emancipation has landed them in a worse economic slavery.

In most cases, victims are unable to liberate themselves because even if they try to escape from their exploiters, where would they go? The last thing a victim wants is to be deported to her home country. She knows she stands a high risk of deportation, or worse, if she attempts to do anything contrary to the wish of her captors. She also blames herself for what happened. This makes most of the victims of human trafficking resign to their fates; reckoning that they have no other option than to continue enduring the unjust treatment until their traffickers deem it fit to grant them freedom.

Oftentimes, it takes a long time to gain freedom. This is due to several factors. In some instances, such as the victims of human smuggling turned human trafficking, the victims are told that they must pay a large amount of money to be freed. There is a "debt" that seemingly can never be paid. In rare cases where the victim is somehow able to repay the money, she would be set free without any proper provision for legalizing her presence in the United States.

Some are freed by the help of others. Some victims take their destinies into their hands and just opted out in desperation, daring the consequences. In other cases, authorities help secure the release of the victims.

As attorneys, it is important to be aware of what situations give rise to human trafficking so that we can properly screen for victims and assist them in applying for immigration relief.

A mistake that many attorneys make is that we do not screen consultations to see if they have been victims of human trafficking. Instead, we wait for victims to show up to our offices and declare, "I am a victim of human trafficking," before we discuss any possible relief with them.

The problem is that human trafficking takes many forms. Oftentimes victims do not know or understand that they have been victims of human trafficking. This is why this book is essential in helping you learn how to identify human trafficking, and then use the T Visa to help clients gain lawful status in the United States.

This book is written as a how-to guide that will furnish you with information about how to assist victims of human trafficking. You'll be guided on how to properly screen for a T Visa in the consultation, analyze the case of each victim of human trafficking, articulate the type of human trafficking of which your client was a victim, and assemble a T Visa case.

We start this book by introducing you to the T Visa, its categories, eligibility, duration, and revocation along with the definitions of the elements of the T Visa. We will then discuss the main scenarios that give rise to human trafficking, and thus T Visa eligibility. We will also highlight the differences between human trafficking and human smuggling. We will give you a guide to help you screen for T Visas as well as how to proceed once you have identified a client as a victim of human trafficking.

Our goal is to help you transform your practice and the lives of your clients by using the often-overlooked legal tool of the T Visa.

# CHAPTER ONE

## WHAT YOU NEED TO KNOW
## ABOUT T VISAS

### What Is A T Visa?

The T visa approval notice, with I-94 attached, is issued by USCIS to allow eligible victims of human trafficking and their qualified relatives to remain in the United States on the provision that they assist law enforcement agencies (LEAs) in the investigation and prosecution the perpetrators of the crime of human trafficking. The T visa approval notice is typically mailed with a plastic EAD work permit valid for 4 years, when requested.

Human trafficking is not a new kind of crime. It has been around for a long time. According to the United States government, as of 2002, an estimated 50,000 people were trafficked in the United States. Most of these are women and children of less than 18 years old.

The majority of victims of human trafficking were smuggled into the US only to find themselves trapped in slavery-like situations. The effort to combat human trafficking and protect its victims brought about the enactment of the Trafficking Victims Reauthorization Act (TVPRA) and the Trafficking Victims Protection Act (TVPA) with accompanying regulations. These laws made it possible to file for a T visa for human trafficking victims. In 2006, Congress amended the Act, which allows for victims to be granted T Visas for 4 years, and to apply for lawful permanent residence after 3 years. There is also a provision to apply prior to the 3 years in certain cases.

## Eligibility for a T Visa

To be eligible for a T visa, an applicant must demonstrate convincing evidence that s/he has been or is a victim of human trafficking. The burden of proof like with most benefits applications filed with USCIS, is a "preponderance of the evidence" meaning 51% or "more likely than not." But, of course, to win a case we must convince the USCIS adjudicator that all criteria have been met. Below is the summary of the criteria:

- The applicant was a victim of human trafficking, which has been defined as "the recruitment, harboring, transportation, provision, or obtaining of a person for labor or services, through the use of force, fraud, or coercion for the purpose of subjection to involuntary servitude, peonage, debt bondage, or slavery." 22 U.S.C.A. §7102 (8)(B).

- The applicant is physically present in the United States "on account of" the trafficking.

- The applicant is willing to report the trafficking and comply with reasonable requests for assistance in the investigation and prosecution of acts of trafficking in persons.

- The applicant would suffer extreme hardship involving severe and unusual harm if returned to his or her home country.

- The following are what would be considered:

  - Age, maturity, and personal circumstances of the T visa applicant

  - The likelihood that the applicant will be re-victimized. It is important to consider this in the light of the fact that the authorities of the applicant's home country may not be willing or able to protect a survivor or human trafficking from re-victimization

- The nature and gravity of the physical and psychological effect of the victimization on the victim

- The likelihood that the applicant will be harmed by traffickers, their relatives, cohorts or syndicates upon return (especially if the applicant is not protected by legal and security system of the foreign country. It should be determined if the extant laws, social practices, or custom of the land to which the applicant is being removed would penalize the applicant because of being a victim)

- The likelihood that the applicant will be exposed to dangers from civil unrest or armed conflict upon return to the home country

- Applicant has a serious physical or mental illness for which s/he will be unable to receive treatment if deported

- The likelihood of the loss of access to the United States criminal justice system as it relates to the incident of a severe form of trafficking in persons.

## Clarifying the Provisions of Eligibility for T Visa

Since the year 2000 when the Trafficking Victims Protection Act made possible the provision of T Visa to grant T nonimmigrant status, permanent residency, or even citizenship, to human trafficking survivors, Department of Homeland Security (DHS) has been in the forefront of ensuring compliance with provisions of the Act. There have been statutory amendments and changes to the rules based on comments from the public or professionals. Some of those changes that went into effect on January 18, 2017, are itemized below.

- The definition and the discussions of the Law Enforcement Agencies (LEAs) have been expanded to include state and local law enforcement agencies.

- The age at which the applicants must comply with any reasonable request for assistance by any LEA to investigate or prosecute a case of trafficking in person has been raised from 15 to 18.

- The T visa filing deadline for those trafficked prior to 10/28/00 has been removed, making it easier for someone who was a victim of trafficking prior to that time, to file for a T visa now.

- An applicant may be exempted from complying with this requirement if due to the physical or psychological trauma, s/he is unable to assist an LEA in investigation and prosecution.

- The definition of "physical presence on account of trafficking" in the United States has been expanded to accommodate those who enter just to participate in an investigation or judicial process that relates to a trafficking case.

- A T-1 principal victim that is under 21 years of age is now allowed to apply for T nonimmigrant status for an unmarried sibling under 18 years, and parents.

- The same is allowed for a T-1 principal applicant *of any age* if unmarried siblings under 18 years of age and/or parents face danger of retaliation from the traffickers on account of the principal T-1 applicant's escape from the trafficking situation or from cooperation with law enforcement.

- A T-1 principal applicant of any age is now allowed to apply for T nonimmigrant status for his or her children (even adult sons and daughters) if the children face a present danger of retaliation from the traffickers on account of the principal T-1 applicant's escape or as a result of the cooperation with an LEA.

- All T-2, T-3, T-4, and T-5 nonimmigrants are now eligible to apply for an adjustment of status in most cases

- It is no longer necessary to ascertain that family members would face extreme hardship if the T-1 applicant is not allowed to remain in the United States, or is deported from the United States before the T-1 visa could be granted

- Extending and limiting the duration of the T immigrant status to four years and allowing extension if an LEA needs it, if there is an exceptional circumstance, or if the application for adjustment of status is still under consideration

- Expanding the definition of sex trafficking to accommodate acts of sex under unusual circumstances without the consent of the victim.

- Making it clear that coercion can take the form of psychological coercion such as threatening deportation, abuse of the legal process, reputational harm, and that sort of thing. The definition of involuntary servitude includes psychological coercion.

In the interest of security and safety, the DHS also included other discretionary changes and clarifications based on experiences that DHS has had with the T visa program since its inception. Here are some of those changes.

- Making clear how USCIS will exercise its authority to give waivers in criminal inadmissibility grounds

- The practice of weighing a "T visa certification" as either primary or secondary to determine "any credible evidence" has been discontinued. Previously, if a T certification form I-914B was not provided, USCIS would consider other evidence as "secondary evidence," but now all evidence can be weighed equally.

- Guidance has been provided on what the "severe form of trafficking in persons means" in cases where the victim has not performed labor, services, or a commercial sex act. A T visa can be obtained for someone who was essentially a victim of attempted trafficking, or conspiracy to traffic, which opens the door for more applications.

- It has addressed the situation where although the trafficking took place outside the United States, it is still possible for the victim to meet the requirement of being physically present

- The T-1 applicant is no longer required to provide three passport-style photographs

## T Visa Categories

One of the benefits of the T Visa is that it allows for so many derivatives, many more than other types of visas. T visas are granted in four or five (or even six) categories, namely T-1 visa, T-2 visa, T-3 visa, T-4 visa, and T-5 visa.

***T-1 visa:*** This can be granted to someone who has been a victim of a severe form of human trafficking and meets all the T Visa criteria.

***T-2 visa:*** A victim of trafficking in person who has already been granted T-1 visa may apply for a T-2 visa for his or her spouse who can otherwise be admissible to the United States of America. This family relationship must have been in existence at the time the principal victim is applying for T-1 nonimmigrant status.

***T-3 visa:*** T-3 visa can be granted to a child of the principal T-1 visa applicant upon demonstrating convincing evidence that the T-3 visa is needed in the best interest of the T-1 visa applicant and the child.

***T-4 visa:*** If the principal victim that has been granted a T-1 visa is a child, a T-4 visa application can be made for his or her parent to be granted a nonimmigrant status.

***T-5 visa:*** T-5 visa can be granted to siblings of the victim that has been granted or has applied for the T-1 visa if such siblings are under 18 and unmarried.

There are other conditions for granting these derivative visas as we will see later. For example, before T-2, T-3, T-4, or T-5 visa can be granted, the applicant must show the sufficient evidence to prove that the person for whom the derivative T visa is being sought is an immediate family member of the T-1 nonimmigrant and is related to him or her as provided for in the category of T visa being applied for.

It is important to demonstrate that the T-1 principal applicant would suffer extreme hardship if the T-2, T-3, T-4, or T-5 visa is not issued to the immediate family member to allow him or her to accompany the principal T-1 visa applicant.

## What about T-6 Status?

While T-2 to T-5 visas are derived from a direct relationship to the principal T-1 nonimmigrant, the T-6 status is derived from a relationship to a T-2, T-3, T-4, or T-5 applicant (someone who has benefitted from or will benefit from being related to the principal T-1 applicant) only if there is "present danger of retaliation."

The table below puts all of this in simpler terms:

| T-1 status | Direct relationship status | T-6 relationship status |
|---|---|---|
| If you are a T-1 principal under 21 years of age | Your spouse can derive T-2 status from your T-1 status | On the basis of the T-2 relationship, your spouse's child of any age may be granted T-6 status |
| If you are a T-1 principal under 21 years of age | Your unmarried child under the age of 21 can derive T-3 status from your T-1 status | On the basis of T-3 relationship, your child's child of any age may be granted T-6 status |
| If you are a T-1 principal under 21 years of age | Your parent can derive T-4 status from your T-1 status | On the basis of the T-4 relationship, your parent' child of any age may be granted T-6 status |
| If you are a T-1 principal under 21 years of age | Your unmarried sibling under the age of 18 can | Based on the T-5 relationship, your sibling's child of |

|  | derive T-5 status from your T-1 status | any age may be granted T-6 status |
|---|---|---|
| If you are a T-1 principal over 21 years of age | Your spouse can derive T-2 status from your T-1 status | Based on the T-2 relationship, your spouse's child of any age may be granted T-6 status |
| If you are a T-1 principal over 21 years of age | Your unmarried child under the age of 21 can derive T-3 status from your T-1 status | Based on the T-3 relationship, your child's child of any age may be granted T-6 status |
| If you are a T-1 principal alien of any age | Your parent can derive T-4 status from your T-1 status | On the basis of the T-4 relationship, your parent' child of any age may be granted T-6 status |
| If you are a T-1 principal alien of any age | Your unmarried sibling under the age of 18 can derive T-5 status from your T-1 status | On the basis of the T-5 relationship, your sibling's child of any age may be granted T-6 status |

It should be noted, however, that for a child of a T-1
nonimmigrant's parent, sibling, spouse, or child to be

granted a T-6 visa, it must be ascertained that the following situations exist:

1. There must be a present danger of retaliation from the traffickers.

2. The derivatives of the T-1 must be currently holding their respective T status, have an application pending the determination and the application will be approved with or before the T-6 derivable from it. From this, it could be deduced that:

   - Not every child of parents who may qualify for T-2, T-3, T-4, or T-5 status is eligible for T-6 status even if the child faces a present danger of retaliation. For example, if a potential T-6 applicant's parent never held the respective T status (perhaps due to the eligibility issue, or availability), the child could not derive a T-6 status from him or her.

3. The ages listed here must be the age as at the time the principal filed the application for T-1 status

4. Marital status of the T-6 applicant does not affect his or her eligibility, and

5. No other relative can derive a T status from the approved T-6 status

6. It is not a "must" for a T-6 applicant's parents to hold a derivative status (T-1, T-2, T-3, T-4, or T-5) before the application for T-6 can be filed. The T-6 category is a provision to be explored only when such a child is in real danger of retaliation. And USCIS understands that different member of a family may be in this danger at different times. By extension, this would be understood to mean:

   - If a T-2 holder dies before his or her T-1 principal (spouse) files an application for T-6 for the spouse's child, the child may still derive an eligibility from the T-2 status

   - Similarly, if a T-4 parent's status lapses without being extended, the T-1 principal could still file for the child's T-6 status based on the parent's T-4 status in the face of a present danger of retaliation

There are a lot of cases that can be used to illustrate all that has been said in this chapter about T visa application, which will give a clearer understanding of the provision T visa. The next chapter will analyze some of those cases with a view to determining the eligibility of an applicant.

## The Rate of T Visa Issuance

Although the issuance of T visas is capped at 5,000 per year, less than 2,000 have been issued directly or through a change of status in any given year. Immigration lawyers are not filing for T visas frequently enough, and we believe that it because they are not trained to ask the right questions during their screenings and consultations.

In the first two quarters of Fiscal Year 2018, USCIS only received 828 T-1 applications. In those two quarters, USCIS approved 324 T-1 applications, and denied 155 (the numbers don't add up because they are talking about a snapshot of what happened in the two quarters, not giving a statistic about the percentage of likelihood of a grant). There are currently an estimated 1500 T-1 applications pending with USCIS, well below the cap of 5000 that could be approved if lawyers filed more good T visa cases. Because USCIS is taking about 10.5 months to adjudicate a T-1 case (or about 3-6 months more if a Request for Evidence was issued and responded to), and because so few lawyers screen for and file T-1 cases, we believe that the number of cases approved in 2018 will be less than 2000. T visa cases are right under our noses, and lawyers are missing out on these opportunities for their clients.

For those who file T-1 applications where derivatives are abroad needing visas to come to the US as derivative family members (e.g. spouse, child, sibling, or parent), see the below chart regarding consular (not USCIS) adjudications of visa stickers.

Consider this fact from the *"Non-immigrant visa statistics"* covering 2003 to 2015 fiscal years retrieved on March 18, 2017, from the United States Department of State.

| Fiscal Year | No. of T-1 visas issued | No. of T-2 visas issued | No. of T-3 visas issued | No. of T-4 visas issued | No. of T-5 visas issued | Total No. T visas issued |
|---|---|---|---|---|---|---|
| 2003 | 0 (however, the reason the number in this column is always zero is that the principal T-1 case must be granted by USCIS in the USA, not DOS/consular officers abroad, while derivative applications in the columns to the right are those granted abroad by consular officers). This chart also does not | 20 | 38 | 0 | 0 | 58 |

| | include derivative applications for those derivatives who are physically present in the USA when approved. | | | | | |
|---|---|---|---|---|---|---|
| 2004 | 0 | 74 | 145 | 0 | 0 | 219 |
| 2005 | 0 | 35 | 65 | 7 | 5 | 112 |
| 2006 | 0 | 11 | 43 | 5 | 1 | 60 |
| 2007 | 0 | 20 | 70 | 5 | 3 | 98 |
| 2008 | 0 | 34 | 132 | 5 | 8 | 179 |
| 2009 | 0 | 8 | 81 | 3 | 3 | 95 |
| 2010 | 0 | 64 | 167 | 7 | 8 | 246 |
| 2011 | 0 | 127 | 258 | 10 | 14 | 409 |
| 2012 | 0 | 151 | 342 | 7 | 17 | 517 |
| 2013 | 0 | 171 | 357 | 22 | 31 | 581 |
| 2014 | 0 | 115 | 370 | 18 | 13 | 516 |
| 2015 | 0 | 111 | 376 | 10 | 10 | 507 |

These figures are compiled from the number of T visas issued at US embassies and consulates *outside the United States*. The chart does not capture the data of victims who changed nonimmigrant status to T status inside the United States after gaining freedom from traffickers, because USCIS process those cases domestically. As you can see, no T-1 visa was issued between 2003 to 2015 at US embassies and consulates, which is likely due to USCIS's interpretation of "present in the US on account of trafficking" that requires that the T-1 applicant be physically in the United States to apply. This is why one set of numbers explains the number of filings and approvals for stateside T-1 applicants, and a separate chart has been provided above regarding derivatives who are outside the US. Just think of how emotional and rewarding it has been for the immigration lawyers to reunite the T-1 survivor with his or her family members who had been stuck abroad. You will want to not only screen for T-1 eligibility, but also screen for whether derivatives can apply to allow for family reunification. As we discussed above, some derivative and T-6 combinations would even allow for a T-1's grandchild or niece to get a T visa!

## Continued Presence

Unique circumstances of the applicant and peculiarities of trafficking cases might make it necessary for an attorney to request "continued presence" for the victim pending the filing, consideration, and approval of the T nonimmigrant status. When a Law Enforcement Agency decides to investigate a human trafficking case, it usually is an extensive and lengthy investigation that can involve multiple law enforcement agencies. For this reason, "continued presence" is provided by the TVPA/TVPRA so that trafficking victims can have access to physical, emotional, and medical support and care, including shelter and other services before their cases are decided as meriting T-visa or removal proceeding. It is a quasi-legal status akin to deferred action since it is a lawful presence but not a non-immigrant nor immigrant status. Continued Presence oftentimes is not granted and/or circumstances would not be right to request it. Usually Continued Presence is obtained in "hot" cases that are recent rescues where DHS was heavily involved, not in "colder" cases where a private practitioner is assisting the victim.

## Duration of T Nonimmigrant Status

Based on the amendment and if it is in practice now, the approved T nonimmigrant status that the victim acquired when s/he is granted the T visa shall expire after 4 years from the date of approval. However, if it is certified by a Federal, State, or local law enforcement official, prosecutor, judge, or other investigating authority or prosecuting activity relating to human trafficking that the victim or immigrant's presence in the USA is necessary for the investigation or prosecution of such activity, the status may be extended.

If the T nonimmigrant status is granted or an extension is approved for a victim or an immigrant, the U.S. Citizenship and Immigration Services (USCIS) shall notify the victim or immigrant when his or her (new) nonimmigrant status will expire. The applicant is required to immediately notify USCIS of any changes in his or her circumstances which may affect eligibility.

Upon receiving such notification from the applicant, the USCIS shall let the victim or immigrant granted a T nonimmigrant status know that s/he needs to apply for adjustment of status in good time, adding that failure to file in such application for adjustment of status to permanent resident naturally results in termination of the victim's T nonimmigrant status at the expiration of the 4-year period, if that status is not extended.

T visa holders who properly apply for the adjustment of status to become a person admitted to permanent residency will be considered eligible for adjustment of status.

## After Issuance of T Status

If the T-status is granted, it will be issued on Form I-797 accompanied by Form I-94 on the bottom third of the page. The implication of the I-94 is that the applicant is lawfully admitted in the United States as a T nonimmigrant for a validity period of four years.

Upon receiving the approval of T-1 status, send the approval letter and work permit to the client with other relevant memos (like how to prepare permanent residency, for example). You must inform the applicant of the limitations of T status and the circumstances for an extension. It should also be noted that for a beneficiary of a T status to apply for status adjustment, he must do that before three years of the approval period. A sample T Visa approval letter is included in the appendix. One of our favorite things to do when giving the T approval to the client, is to ask if they want to go ahead and start their green card process immediately! More on this later.

***Employment Authorization:*** USCIS will also issue an initial Employment Authorization Document (EAD card) together with T status approval to allow your client to work legally in the U.S. for the full duration of the validity period given on the Form I-797 (usually 4 years). If for any reason, the EAD is not granted for the full period, or it was granted but is destroyed, lost, or stolen, Forms I-765 and G-28 (if presented by counsel) can be used to file for an extension.

The process is similar for derivative T status holders to file for employment authorization. Each one should submit the Form I-765 with the I-914 Supplement A (if in the US). If the T derivative consular processes abroad, and is admitted on a T visa to the US, the I-765 is filed after entering the US and the work permit is usually issued a few months later.

***Adjustment of Status to Permanent Residency:*** Many lawyers are so excited that their first T visa has been granted, that they forget their client might also be eligible to try for a green card immediately! After three years of approval, *or after completion of the investigation/prosecution of acts of trafficking* (whichever comes first), the principal T-1 may adjust his or her status to permanent residency (obtaining "LPR" or "green card"). Up to 5,000 principal T visa holders can adjust status each fiscal year, according to INA 245(l)(4).

To be eligible for a Green Card as a principal T-1 nonimmigrant, you must meet the following conditions:

- You were lawfully admitted to the United States as a T-1 nonimmigrant;

- You continue to hold T-1 nonimmigrant status at the time of applying for a Green Card;

- You have maintained continuous physical presence in the United States for either:

  a) A continuous period of at least 3 years since the date when you were first lawfully admitted as a T-1 nonimmigrant; or

  b) A continuous period during the trafficking investigation or prosecution that the U.S. Attorney General has determined is now complete, whichever period of time is shorter (a or b).

- You have shown good moral character since first being admitted as a T-1 nonimmigrant and during the entire time your I-485 is pending; and

♦ You meet one of the following:

- You have complied with any reasonable request for assistance in the investigation or prosecution of acts of trafficking since first being admitted as a T-1 nonimmigrant and until USCIS makes a decision on your Form I-485;

- You would suffer extreme hardship involving unusual and severe harm if you were removed from the United States; or

- You were under 18 years of age at the time of the trafficking.

In addition, before you can obtain a Green Card, you must be admissible to the United States as a lawful permanent resident. Otherwise you must have been granted a waiver by USCIS of any waivable grounds of inadmissibility that apply to you. Note that grounds waived for the original T, are considered waived for the green card, so you only need a new waiver if the T client has done something else that would trigger inadmissibility.

As soon an application for T status has been filed, it is a good idea to advise clients to begin keeping documents that can prove their continuous physical presence in the

U.S. such as rent or utility payments, medical bills, prescription history, cell phone bills, paystubs, library history, and/or affidavits from clergy. Continuing therapy and medical treatment can help bolster the green card case later on, as well.

## When to File for the Adjustment of Status

Generally speaking, the rule is that an individual must have been holding T status for three years before filing for the adjustment of status. An exemption is that T visa holder can file as soon as granted T status if s/he can prove that the investigation or prosecution is concluded. The most acceptable proof of that is a letter from the Department of Justice (DOJ) that confirms that the investigation is closed. The letter is not that hard to get! You can email DOJ for it, and they will email you back (currently in about 6-12 weeks). In some cases, our clients reported the trafficking through our firm; an incident report was never created; the LEA never certified our client for a T; there was no further investigation beyond our attempt to report; and yet when the T is granted, we can still email DOJ and get that Early Adjustment letter sent to us, so that our client can move forward with an I-485. This is a huge benefit to your client!

After a T Visa is granted, try reaching out right away to the DOJ to request the letter confirming that the investigation is closed. This is a great strategy to help your client be able to apply for adjustment of status as quickly as possible. In the appendix, we have included a sample request to the DOJ for the letter. And, while you are waiting on that DOJ email to come back to you with the letter, you can also move forward with preparing your I-485 application so that when the letter arrives, you are ready to submit your green card case for the client. You may also want to include a c-0-9 EAD and I-131 advance parole travel document application as part of the green card filing, in case your client needs to travel for urgent humanitarian reasons while the green card case is pending (but the client circumstances, immigration and criminal history, and other factors will determine whether it's just better to wait until the green card is issued, for international travel).

Let's say the trafficking prosecution is still ongoing and so it's not a good time to pursue Early Adjustment. In that case, your client can apply for the green card after holding T status for 3 years, as long as the other requirements (like good moral character, etc.) are met. Because a T visa is usually granted for 4 years, the employment authorization of the applicant and his derivative family members is dependent on his or her T status. It's important to get started on that green card case (plus those for family members) well in advance of time before the end of his or her three-year period of continuous T-1 status, so that you are ready to file shortly after the third anniversary of T status has been completed. Also, it's important to read the rules and regs on T visa adjustment, and please remember that many of the rules are different from U visa adjustment. Don't let the similarities between Ts and Us fool you into thinking everything is the same, because it's not.

If a client does not file for the adjustment of status within the required amount of time, the T status will be terminated at the expiration of the T approval notice. A good practice is to remind clients in writing of the plan, and to encourage them to get a consultation shortly after T approval to go over their rights, privileges, and plans for the future, so that they are aware of what they will need to do to keep T status and have a path to a green card.

## Revocation of T Visa

It is possible for a victim that has been granted the T nonimmigrant status to have his or her visa revoked. To prevent a future misinterpretation of information, the nonimmigrant is expected to immediately notify the USCIS if there are changes in his condition if such changes have contradicted the information supplied by the nonimmigrant when filing the application for T status and are deemed to have any effects on the eligibility for T status. Otherwise, USCIS reserves the power of revocation of T nonimmigrant status. The following are the grounds for such revocations.

i. If it's discovered that the T nonimmigrant has violated one of the requirements of the T visa.

ii. If it's found out that the approval of the T visa application was in error or the process of approval violated the applicable laws or regulations.

iii. If a law enforcement agency (LEA) with the appropriate jurisdiction notifies the USCIS that the victim has bluntly refused to give the necessary assistance during the process of investigation and prosecution of the human trafficking offender. The LEA shall be the one empowered and authorized to detect and investigate the kind of this immigrant's case and the LEA is required to provide in writing a detailed explanation of its assertion against the victim

iv. If the LEA withdraws its earlier endorsement of the immigrant's application or denies the statements made in it, and notifies the USCIS in writing, giving a detailed explanation of its position.

v. If a T-2 (spouse) has obtained a final divorce from the T-1 principal immigrant, his or her T-2 nonimmigrant status may be revoked.

In any of the above cases, the USCIS is required to send a notice of intent to revoke the status to the T nonimmigrant with an explanation of the reason.

A district director is empowered to revoke the approval of a T nonimmigrant status at any time (before or after the expiration of the validity of the status). Before then, however, he will notify the nonimmigrant of the intent to revoke his or her status. This notice shall be in writing and shall include in detail the grounds for revocation and the time period within which the nonimmigrant is allowed to rebut it. The victim is expected to submit his or her evidence in rebuttal within 30 days. USCIS could take weeks or months to make a decision as to whether to revoke T status.

Within 15 days after the USCIS has given the nonimmigrant the notice of revocation, the immigrant may appeal the decision. If the revocation of status of a T-1 nonimmigrant occurs, all family members who derive their T nonimmigrant status from the victim (T-2, T-3, T-4, or T-5) would forfeit their own T nonimmigrant status. If T-1 status is revoked, pending derivative applications will be denied.

Section 240 of the Immigration & Nationality Act empowers DHS to institute a removal proceeding against a T nonimmigrant status holder without revocation. This can be done if it is discovered after admission that the nonimmigrant is involved in a conduct or comes to be in a condition that was hidden from USCIS before the T status was granted. For instance, an applicant may have misrepresented material facts in his or her application for the nonimmigrant visa.

To avoid the risk of denial, revocation of status, or even removal proceeding, it is important to be truthful and refrain from misrepresentation of information on any T visa application. In a "hot" case where the trafficking investigation and prosecution is ongoing, it helps to have a lawyer helping the client through the cooperation process, along with getting trafficking related psychological, housing and other services to the client to support the individual through this difficult process. While many T visa applicant reports to law enforcement don't even result in a thorough investigation or even a response from the LEA, it's important to know the revocation rules and communicate them to your client just in case the investigation picks up later on.

# CHAPTER TWO

## DEFINING HUMAN TRAFFICKING

───────◆──────○──────◆───────

Before we delve into the how-to's of the T Visa, let's first define human trafficking.

### Defining Human Trafficking

The T visa is available only to victims "severe forms of trafficking in persons." What constitutes a severe form of trafficking? Defining "severe forms of trafficking in person," the TVPA says it includes sex trafficking and "the recruitment, harboring, transportation, provision, or obtaining of a person, through the use of force, fraud, or coercion, for the purpose of subjection to involuntary servitude, peonage, debt bondage, slavery, or commercial sex" —8 CFR 214.11(a)

In order to meet the definition of trafficking, you must demonstrate:

1. The person was recruited, harbored, transported, provided or obtained

2. Through force, fraud, or coercion

3. For the purpose of being subjected to a commercial sex act, involuntary servitude, peonage, debt bondage, or slavery (note: it could be all of these, or just one).

4. Note that the statutory definition doesn't require a victim to have actually performed labor, services or a commercial sex act to be considered a victim of a severe form of trafficking. Attempt or conspiracy may be sufficient.

## Defining Sex Trafficking, Involuntary Servitude, Peonage, Debt Bondage, and Slavery

The TVPRA and corresponding regulations provide helpful definitions to help delineate these definitions.

● ***Commercial sex act.*** This is any sex act on account of which anything of value is given to or received by the person. For example, a person could be held hostage over a period of time and raped, and given food or phone calls in exchange for the sexual slavery. that would be something of value, even if not money, and could constitute a commercial sex act for the purpose of demonstrating human trafficking. Note that the labor trafficking prong directly uses the phrase "for the purpose of," whereas the sex trafficking prong of the statutory definition does not. The term "sex trafficking" does not just mean recruitment, harboring, transportation, provision or obtaining, but it also means *patronizing or solicitation* of a person for the purpose of a commercial sex act. Although the statute requires the commercial sex act to be "induced," the law doesn't require that the inducement be "successful' in order for the victim to satisfy the definition of commercial sex trafficking. For example, by negotiating with the father of a minor, a trafficker may attempt to stimulate or cause the minor to engage in sexual activity with him. This would meet the definition of commercial sex trafficking. Also, note that because minors can't consent to sex, no "force, fraud or coercion" prong must be met. With adults, you will need to explain how force, fraud or coercion resulted in the commercial sex act (or attempt or conspiracy).

♦ *Involuntary servitude:* This is a condition of servitude induced by means of any scheme, plan, or pattern intended to cause a victim to believe that, if s/he didn't enter into or continue into such condition, that person or another person would suffer serious harm or physical restraint. This includes a condition of servitude in which the victim is forced to work for the defendant by the use or threat of physical restraint or physical injury, or by the use or threat of coercion through law or the legal process. This definition encompasses those cases in which the defendant holds the victim in servitude by placing the victim in fear of such physical restraint or injury or legal coercion." 8 C.F.R. § 214.11(a). Most of our labor trafficking cases will have involuntary servitude, whether it is a case related to how the person came to America, or one where the person was brought into bad work conditions many years later (unconnected to the original entry).

- **Debt bondage:** In such circumstances, victims are told that they have a debt that they must pay off before being released (sometimes it could be the cost of smuggling a victim to the United States). However, victims are perpetually put in debt bondage as there would be no specific time and terms that the debt will or can be canceled or paid off. The victims are then subjected to forced labor such as cleaning, cooking, carrying things, and sex acts, all for which they are not paid.

- ◆ ***Peonage:*** Human trafficking can also take the shape of peonage, which employs the same tactics used in the era of slave trade. It is an involuntary servitude that is based on a real or alleged debt. The "debt" often includes the alleged cost of bringing that person into the United States. Traffickers often use coercion to make victims feel that they "owe" the trafficker their life, their wages, their family's health, or lots of money.

## Defining Force, Fraud, and Coercion

- ◆ ***Force:*** New Webster's Dictionary and Thesaurus defines "force" as "violence, compulsion, or constraint exerted upon or against a person or thing." In human trafficking, force often involves the use of physical violence such as hitting, kicking, punching, beating, rape, and more.

- ◆ ***Fraud:*** New Webster's Dictionary and Thesaurus defines fraud as "the use of deception for unlawful gain or unjust advantage." In trafficking situations, this can translate to false promises of employment, working conditions, or wages. In human smuggling turned human trafficking, fraud is used when the person is promised a safe, quick passage and release upon entering the United States, and then upon arriving, the person is held against his or her will for days, weeks, months, or even years.

♦ **Coercion:** This means forcing or compelling someone to do something against his or her will. It involves the use of threats of severe harm or physical restraint against any person to make the person believe that failure to perform a stipulated act would bring about great harm to the victim or his or her loved ones. Coercion can also involve the use or abuse or threatened abuse of legal process.

- The trafficking statute and regulations define coercion as "threats of serious harm to or physical restraint against any person; any scheme, plan or pattern intended to cause a person to believe that failure to perform an act would result in serious harm to or physical restraint against any person; or the abuse or threatened abuse of the legal process." 8 C.F.R. 214.11(a); 22 U.S.C. 7102(2). The statute on forced labor defines "serious harm" as any harm "whether physical or nonphysical, including psychological, financial or reputational harm, that is sufficiently serious, under all the surrounding circumstances, to compel a reasonable person of the same background and in the same circumstances to perform or to continue performing labor or services in order to avoid incurring that harm." 18 U.S.C. 1589(c)(2).

The table below gives a summary of what is required to meet the definition of trafficking. You can refer to this when analyzing a case:

| Process | Means | Purpose (End) |
|---|---|---|
| Recruitment<br><br>Transportation<br><br>Transfer<br><br>Harboring<br><br>The way of receiving victims | Threat<br><br>Coercion<br><br>Force<br><br>Fraud<br><br>Abduction<br><br>Deception<br><br>Abuse of legal process<br><br>Abuse of power | Exploitation which may include<br><br>Prostitution and other kinds of sexual exploitation<br><br>Forced labor and services<br><br>Physical abuse<br><br>Slavery and similar practices<br><br>Involuntary servitude<br><br>Inflicting physical injury |

Putting all of these into perspective, proving a case of human trafficking to secure a T visa for an adult victim will require that you establish any of these three elements among other things.

♦ **Trafficking process:** The process must include any of recruitment, transferring, transporting, and harboring the victim against his expressed or implied wish

- **Means of trafficking:** The person must have been moved by threat, coercion, deception, fraud, intimidation, abduction, or abuse of power

- **Purpose of trafficking:** This must include any of prostitution, pornography, sexual exploitation, forced labor, violence, peonage, involuntary servitude, and bondage

# CHAPTER THREE

## T VISA SCENARIOS

———◆———○———◆———

Immigration practitioners must be able to recognize a case of human trafficking. It doesn't matter what kind of immigration law you practice, whether you practice mostly business immigration or whether you do mostly family-based immigration. It is essential to be able to screen for possible T Visas. Most clients who are victims of human trafficking do not show up at your office and state such. Again, many trafficked persons do not even fully understand that what happened to them was human trafficking. Instead, they chalk it up to a bad employer or a misunderstanding or something that they "deserve" for some reason (i.e. entering the US unlawfully). As such, your role as the attorney is critical in drawing out information to determine whether a potential client has been a victim of human trafficking.

People will leave out entire stories of human trafficking because no one ever asked them if their employer forced them to have sex and work without pay. We as lawyers often assume something like that didn't happen if the client hasn't told us. But our job in a consultation is to ask those questions, and find out. When we don't ask, a trafficking survivor with an awesome case will walk away undetected. Business immigration lawyers are equally urged to screen their clients for trafficking because there are a lot of scams related to business and student visas that make up the $150 billion trafficking industry we are faced with today.

Most immigration practitioners do not screen for the T visa because they do not understand what constitutes trafficking. Below are some of the typical scenarios for human trafficking that can guide you as you speak with potential clients:

1. A "coyote" (human smuggler) promises an unsuspecting immigrant a safe journey to the United States at a low cost. The coyote says that the immigrant will have a quick walk through the desert, about 2 hours or so, and then will be released to his family upon arriving in the US. In exchange, the victim pays $1,500 to be smuggled

to the US. Once the victim is in full custody of the traffickers, he is forced and threatened to cook, clean and perform other works a servant does, in an abandoned trailer for weeks or months. Meanwhile, other victims are being pimped out to other coyotes who in turn make the immigrants do whatever the other coyotes demand, such as carry in exotic animals, carry water and backpacks for the coyotes, prepare and serve them food, and more. Other victims are forced to carry drugs while others just walk. The immigrants are not paid for this. They are barely given any food or water. Fraud is used in the form of the promise of safe passage and other weapons of subjugation like coercion (threats) are used to keep their victims under their control.

This is a scenario of human trafficking because there is unpaid labor obtained through fraud and coercion. It may sound strange, but think about it: There was no minimum wage paid for the cooking and cleaning; there were unsafe "working" conditions; and the victims who were pimped out were also subjected to commercialized sex without payment. These individuals began with a border crime (smuggling) situation, but it turned into human trafficking (a crime against humans) when through fraud and coercion, unpaid labor and/or commercialized sex were forced upon the immigrants. Also note, this could have happened to a US citizen – and it does happen every day. The reason we speak of it in an immigration context is simply because the focus of this book is T visas for trafficking survivors.

2. There is an agent in India who charges $50,000 to smuggle an Indian woman to the United States. Knowing the full legal implications of what she is doing, she agrees to be smuggled. En route inside the boat, the agent begins to abuse her, which she was not expecting. She is starved, beaten, and threatened alongside others who are being smuggled like her. When she arrives in the US, instead of releasing her, she is left with a family where she is to work for 6 months as a babysitter. This is work that is to repay the debt that her "agent" incurred during her travel. In a bid to further exploit her, she is brought to New York and given to another "agent," who tells her that the trip costs more than she had paid, and she must work with another family to pay off the balance for them. She has no choice other than to comply since she has no language skill, she has no idea of how to seek help. She has been coerced and defrauded. The family she works with does not pay her and she is told that she's lucky to have a place to stay and food to eat. Her food is poorly rationed.

She has no allowance, and the kids don't even realize that she is working for them against her will. As soon as they are through with her, the agent will transfer her to another family. This has been her experience from family to family until she meets someone who can help her arrange for an escape.

In a case like this, the Indian woman is a survivor of labor trafficking. Try to forget for a moment how she entered the US, and focus instead in your mind on how she was, through coercion, made to work without minimum wage. Often the "room and board" trick is applied to the nanny/babysitter context and the family will tell the nanny that she's getting a better deal with them because on nanny wages alone, she could not afford a good home and food. The law says otherwise. The law in the US provides for wage and hour rules that require payment in this context, and they have put her into a situation where there is debt bondage and involuntary servitude. There is no clear way for her to escape the debt. A person like this may never tell this story, unless she is asked. Our job as immigration lawyers is to complete a consultation by starting at the beginning of her journey and screening all employment situations in her entire US history as well as her journey to the US. A case like this could still be reported today even if many years have passed, and T visa should be viable.

Let's look at scenario #3:

3. There is a young woman who falls in love with a man who promises that he can bring her to the United States and give her a better life. He promises her a job in the United States, good pay, and safety. The man hides her in the trunk of his car to smuggle her in. Upon arriving in the United States, the man begins to beat her. He pimps her out to his friends and forces her to have sex with whomever he demands. He forces her to tend to his every whim and demand. She must cook for him, clean, and more. He beats her, threatens her, and more. She is not allowed to work outside of the home, except for when he approves it, and that is a form of economic control. When she does work outside of the home, she is required to turn over every cent of her earnings.

In this case, it would be a T visa even without the commercialized sex, since he kept her in an involuntary servitude situation. Did you know that the 13th Amendment to our U.S. constitution was debated as to how it would impact marriage relationships, by prohibiting involuntary servitude through coercion or force by men against their partners or wives? A civil constitutional claim, as well as a criminal trafficking claim, as well as domestic violence claims, could be brought against this woman's trafficker. So many immigration lawyers think that only a U visa is available and that in the context of this hypothetical, a woman would not be able to apply for a U visa because the abuse wasn't reported. *However, she can still report now, and as you will see later, apply for a T visa even if she does not have a T visa certification.*

At the time of this writing, if a T visa option is available for a client, it will often be the best choice even if the crime was reported and a U visa is viable, simply because T visas are processed much more quickly than U visas. However, because T visas don't have "indirect victim certification" options, and because there are different derivative options with Ts and Us, it's important for the attorney to consider both T and U visa options for a client. Perhaps the most important takeaway is that the immigration lawyer should not only look at a victimization case through the prism of a U visa analysis, and instead we must all consider the "T visa lens" as a critical screening method for every immigration consultation. You can look at the world with your "U visa glasses," but you should also put on a pair of "T visa glasses" when screening clients.

Let's look at another scenario that has nothing to do with how the person entered the US, since we don't want to only think about T visas in the context of smuggling or visa violations. I call this the "Hansel and Gretel" example.

4. Hansel and Gretel, from the common fairy tale, are wandering through the forest and discover a gingerbread cottage full of candies. Tired and hungry, they begin to nosh. A witch emerges from the delicious looking cottage and invites them in, with the promise of nice beds and a hot bath. They happily enter, but the witch throws Hansel in a cage and forces Gretel to become her slave. Gretel is not free to leave, and cooks, cleans, and otherwise serves the witch, who feeds her and Hansel until one day they escape. Through force, fraud and coercion, Gretel has become a victim of human trafficking as she has become a slave and labors daily under the witch's threats. Interestingly, Hansel is not a direct victim because he is not being forced to work. Hansel is just being fattened up in the cage to be eaten – so he is a hostage, but not subjected to forced labor or commercialized sex. Hansel is a tool in the witch's coercion, because Gretel is afraid to escape and leave him there. If I were their lawyer, I would probably argue that Hansel is part of the greater conspiracy or attempt to traffic, and I might try a

T visa for both of them. Or, I may just file a derivative T (sibling visa) application for Hansel.

Are you laughing and crying yet? Let's turn this fairy tale into an example of real-world labor trafficking.

5. Hansel and Gretel find a job at a dry cleaner. It seems like a great job, and they are undocumented immigrants who came to the US a few years ago on the visa waiver program from Germany (but again, it really doesn't matter how they came to the US – let's focus on what happens next). They are excited to do this dry-cleaning job because they can buy all the gingerbread they want with their wages from ironing shirts and dresses. When they start, the pay is $8.50/hour and they work 40 hours a week. But then, the boss says that business is bad, and some checks bounce. They are told they will be paid later as soon as profits pick up. Then, more checks bounce. Sometimes they are paid, sometimes not. The overtime is never paid and that's because the boss says they are managing the store, though they are not really managing things and are mostly just ironing clothes and cleaning things. When they complain about their checks, they are told false promises to pay, so they keep coming back to work. Each night, they go to their home. Each morning, they

work. They seem free to leave, but they feel like they can't find another job. The manager has called them "illegals" before. They are afraid that the manager would turn them into the police if they tried to quit.

This is a "gingerbread" house T visa case otherwise known as "domestic trafficking" because they are being coerced and tricked into working without pay, or with only partial pay, in violation of wage and hour laws. They live in an "invisible prison" where they are not really free to leave. This case could be reported to the Dept. of Labor and a T visa may be obtained. It is not "international trafficking" because it has nothing to do with how they got to the US, but rather, they are in the US present on account of human trafficking due to the promise of a paying job in their town, where unpaid labor was obtained through fraud and coercion. These cases are regularly reported to DOL by email to initiate an investigation. Often a site visit will happen where many other violations, like OSHA violations and pretextual terminations based on gender or race, will be discovered. If you collaborate with a good employment law /plaintiff's lawyer, these cases often will have a nice civil lawsuit companion and your client may seek damages, but sometimes the case happened so long ago, or other factors will have occurred that your main relief will simply be reporting and obtaining the T visa.

On the surface, each of these cases may look like a mere case of human smuggling or simple exploitation, or just "crime." For the cases that involve smuggling, do not conflate smuggling with trafficking. Rather, smuggling is just the start of the story as to how forced labor or commercialized sex took place (human trafficking). For the cases that involve labor violations and have nothing to do with whether the person came to the US legally or illegally, again, your focus must be determining whether there was some kind of slavery, involuntary servitude, debt bondage, peonage, etc., as a result of the force, fraud or coercion by the employer/trafficker.

As each example shows, a closer consideration of the working conditions—the nature of work, how they were made to work and how their consent was obtained-- indicates that each of the victims has been trafficked.

There are common trends in the scenarios above. They should be looked for in all cases of human trafficking, and one or more of them should be present in a case. Otherwise, the case might not be strong enough to give the victim the eligibility for a T nonimmigrant status. Consider the implications of the trends in the main scenarios.

- **Job:** The victims are usually promised that they would be given a decent job, better than the ones they are doing in their home country. Yes, they will have job to do, but the conditions will be a far cry from what was promised. They will have to work for unduly long hours or be subjected to forced labor without pay. Some of the other jobs you would find the victims of human trafficking being used for as forced labor are in agriculture, fishery, mining, construction, logging, factory work (e.g. packaging, food processing, and garments), domestic servants, drug runners, janitorial services, pet care, babysitting and so on.

- **Domestic violence:** The victims are usually subjected to forced labor in a house by an intimate partner. They are often not allowed to work outside of the home, or if they do, they must turn over all their earnings to the trafficker/ abuser. Resistance is usually met with violence or the threat of violence to themselves, their children, or to their relatives. They are also under the constant threat of being exposed to "immigration." The trafficking element is often overlooked in cases of domestic violence. It's important to delve deeper beyond just the acts of violence themselves and ask the victim what s/he had to do on a daily basis in the home and what rights s/he had to refuse to do the work. Also, a domestic violence based T visa case could be related to a person who was brought to the US by her abuser, but it may also be one where the person didn't meet her abuser until long after she came to the US. Lawyers are also "under-screening" men and boys for domestic violence and sexual assault. Remember that there is often deep shame involved in these cases, and you will need to screen carefully and develop a trusting relationship with your client in order to get all the facts.

♦ **Sex trafficking:** The victims often find themselves with no other choice than to be subjected to commercial sex. The pay for the "service" rendered does not even come to them directly. If the victims ever get any pay at all, it is a very small portion of it from the traffickers at the traffickers' discretion and not because of any agreement. Often with sex trafficking, lawyers only think of prostitution. However, coyotes often have forced women to have sex as part of the "payment" for taking them to the US, even though that was never part of the smuggling deal. That can be categorized as both sex and labor trafficking in many instances. So we may ask a client if they were ever "abused or threatened" by a coyote to start digging into this potential case.

Although trafficking for forced labor is still being studied to gain more insight into it, trafficking for sexual exploitation has been the most common form of human trafficking. This explains why women and young girls are more vulnerable. The process of recruiting girls and women into sex trafficking has a common pattern, which includes but are not limited to;

   i.  A false promise of a decent job in the United States

   ii. A fake marriage proposal which would later turn into a bondage situation

   iii. A scheme by boyfriends, husbands and other relatives to have the victim sold as a commercial sex worker in the United States, and

   iv. Being kidnapped by traffickers who the victims are often very familiar with. These may be friends, neighbors, a friend of friends, boyfriends, acquaintances, and family friends who the victim has grown to trust

● **Smuggling turned trafficking:** This is when an agreement is reached to smuggle someone into the United States, but then the person being smuggled is forced into work against his or her will. This work can be forced labor such as cooking, cleaning, working in the fields, sex work, restaurant work, or more. Basically, it starts as smuggling and then turns into any of the details listed above. It is easy to overlook this form of relief, yet it is critical to explore with every person who entered the United States unlawfully. Is very crucial which should be carefully checked because if care is not taken, there can be some sort of confusion.

Human smuggling and human trafficking are two clearly different crimes. Nevertheless, smuggling is being used by traffickers to lure their unsuspecting victims into what they never planned for. Although the person being smuggled agreed to commit a crime (entering the US illegally), he may still get trafficked instead of or while being smuggled in. Thus, smuggling, which is already a criminal activity *by accomplices*, can turn into trafficking, another activity *against accomplices*.

Consider the table below that shows what to look for to distinguish trafficking from smuggling.

| Human Trafficking | Human Smuggling |
| --- | --- |
| It is a crime against a person | It is a crime against a border |
| Victims can be either United States citizens or foreign nationals | It always involves foreign nationals |
| It is based on exploitation | It involves only transportation |
| It requires no movement | It requires crossing a border |
| It is involuntary | It is voluntarily submitted to |
| **Hostage for ransom:** If someone who paid to be smuggled into another country is held hostage or held for ransom and abused, and raped, or tortured until s/he pays a smuggling or ransom fee and is thereafter compelled into forced labor or commercial sex, the person HAS BECOME a victim of trafficking. | **Hostage for ransom:** If someone who paid to be smuggled into another country is held hostage or held for ransom and abused, and raped, or tortured until s/he pays a ransom or smuggling fee but is not compelled to do any sort of labor, the person IS NOT a victim of trafficking (without more). |

The key to look for in the cases of smuggling turned trafficking is whether *forced labor* was involved. Mistreatment and bad conditions are not enough to make a smuggling situation a trafficking situation.

# PUT IT INTO PRACTICE!

## Analyzing T Visa Scenarios

In many cases, a T visa client will come to an attorney's office with some ideas in mind of what kind of legal relief s/he qualifies for. In most cases, the potential clients will not clearly identify themselves as survivors of human trafficking. This is especially true when it comes to human smuggling turned human trafficking; survivors do not usually even know that it is human trafficking. It is the attorney's job to screen for and analyze their case in the lens of human trafficking to determine whether the potential client is a victim of human trafficking or not.

Let's analyze a few cases:

## Case 1:

Around February 2014, a man approached a boy in his home and made an offer to him to bring him to the United States to find a better life. Since the boy and his family were living in poverty, he agreed to follow this man who he believed was helping him. After they crossed the border, the man abandoned the boy and tried to extort money from his family using the threat that if they refused to pay, their son might not return home safely.

## Can this victim apply for a T Visa?

No. There is no forced labor. The man used fraud to bring the boy to the United States, however he was never forced to do any work for the man. Thus, this is not a case of human trafficking.

## Case 2:

The boy above is completely alone and lost at the border. He is approached by a woman who appears to be about 32 years old and fair-skinned. She offers to help the boy and says that she needs the contact information of his family to tell them that he is okay. She says that she will bring him to a safe place and help him get a job. Because she "looks American," the boy trusts her and goes with her.

The boy was taken to a fenced house in an area near McAllen, Texas which is not far from the Mexican border. There were male guards in the house along with a group of other immigrants. The lady leaves him there with the armed men and other migrants. While there, he is forced to walk back and forth between certain destinations carrying bags for the men. He is told that he is not allowed to open the bags under any circumstances. He is told that he will be beaten if he does not deliver the bags or if he tries to open them. He is told that he will be beaten "or worse" if he tries to escape. Other migrants in the home are forced to do the same.

Fortunately for this victim, immigration authorities came into the home and did a "bust." The boy was taken away to a youth-detention facility by immigration. He told the authorities about what happened. He was later reunited with his sister in North Carolina.

## Can this victim apply for a T Visa?

Yes. Here are some important considerations:

1. He was transported to the United States using fraud or deception (the promise of safety and a better job)

2. Force and coercion were used to do a job he did not agree to do (he had to carry those bags to certain destinations or be harmed). Per the definition of coercion, he was under "the threat of serious harm to or physical restraint against any person; any scheme, plan or pattern intended to cause a person to believe that failure to perform an act would result in serious harm to or physical restraint against any person."

3. He is physically present in the United States on account of trafficking in persons

4. He was willing to help in investigating and prosecuting the traffickers as he had already described the leader of the group

## Case 3:

In August 2013, a 19-year-old girl who is a native of El Salvador planned to travel to the United States with a "coyote" or smuggler who promised her that she would be able to enter the US from Reynosa, Tamaulipas, Mexico without inspection. She paid $2,000 with a promise that would pay an additional $3,000 to the smuggler upon arrival in Houston, Texas.

When they arrived in Reynosa, her smugglers kept her in "stash house" for three days. She was raped by one of her smugglers at the house. She was not allowed to go out. She later overheard the smugglers discussing what they planned to do to her. She heard them saying that when they succeed in crossing her to McAllen, many men would "use her," and they would earn a lot of money from her. After understanding that the smugglers intended to force her into commercial sex in Texas, she decided to escape.

However, she realized the smugglers had bases on both sides of the border as she had heard them discussing their friends on both sides. Yet, she determined to take the risk and run away, choosing to face death rather than being forced into commercial sex.

She was able to escape one day when her smugglers thought she was in the restroom. She ran out of the compound before the other members of the group could pursue her. When she reached the Rio Grande, she tried to wade through the deep water, but she could not because it was too deep. A Zeta gang member agreed to push her across on a raft after collecting all the money she had. The only option she was left with was to cross the border to the United States.

She was apprehended by the U.S. Border Patrol at the Rio Grande almost immediately and was put in removal proceedings. Meanwhile, she had been supplying information that would lead to the arrest of the smugglers in Texas.

## Can this victim apply for a T Visa?

Yes, on the following grounds which satisfy the provision of the Trafficking Victims Act:

1. She was a victim of "severe forms of trafficking in person" in that her traffickers intended to use her for commercial sex by means of force, fraud, and coercion. They wanted to make money by giving her to men to have sex with her which means that "a commercial sex act" is planned to be "induced by force."

2. She is physically present in the United States or at the port-of-entry on account of trafficking. When she arrived at Reynosa, Mexico, a border

town, her smugglers were already finalizing plans to make money from forcing her to work as a commercial sex worker. As provided by 8 CFR 214.11(g)(2), USCIS may consider "circumstances attributable to the trafficking in persons situation such as trauma, injury, lack of resources, or travel documents that have been seized by the traffickers." This section might be invoked to make a strong case for her.

3. She had complied and is complying with a law enforcement agency's reasonable requests for assistance in investigation and prosecution of traffickers. She has been giving them the needed information.

4. She would suffer extreme hardship in form of re-victimization by her traffickers if removed. Her traffickers are on both sides of the border (Mexico and US) as well as in her home country of El Salvador. Her young age (19) deserves consideration.

The case above is an interesting one because it would present a challenge for attorneys to prove that she had actually been a victim of trafficking and that her presence in the US is due to trafficking, not another crime. But taking a critical look through all the definitions of elements of trafficking and analyzing her personal circumstance, it would be clear that this was a T Visa case. We would expect USCIS to scrutinize the case heavily on the "on account of trafficking" section, and that would need to be carefully briefed.

## Case 4:

A young lady of Tutsi descent from Burundi arrived in Dallas, Texas from her country on about September 1, 2010, on a B1/B2 visa. She planned to meet up with a man who she met online. They fell in love through online chats and long phone conversations. Her hope was that they would meet in person and possibly marry. He made all of the travel arrangements and held all her travel documents. He had romanced her and promised her that her immigration status would be adjusted in the United States once she arrived.

The day after their arrival, the man told her that she had to work to pay back all he had spent to bring her to the United States. He told her that the work she was to do was to have sex with men that would be coming to their house. She was confused and asked about the love that they had created and the marriage that they were planning, but he said that he didn't care. He said that he wanted her to work to pay him back for all of the money that he had spent on her before they could even consider anything else.

That day, a man arrived at their house and the trafficker told the woman that she was going to have to have sex with him. She resisted. The trafficker restrained her so that the man would have his way with her. After that, her trafficker showed her a gun and threatened to kill her if she ever again tried to resist his clients who wanted to have sex with her.

It happened several more times. She finally was able to escape. Once she got free, she was apprehended by ICE. After hearing her case, ICE determined that she was a victim of trafficking and she continued to assist them by supplying information that can lead to the arrest, investigation, and prosecution of her trafficker. She wants justice.

## Can this victim apply for a T Visa?

It is clear from the circumstances of this case that she is eligible for a T Visa on the following grounds:

1.  She was a victim of a severe form of trafficking in persons. This is because her trafficker was using her as a commercial sex worker against her will.

2.  He used fraud to bring her to the US by stating that they were going to get married. He used coercion or force by threatening her with serious harm and even death, and by restraining her from resisting performing the required sex acts.

3.  She is physically present in the United States on account of trafficking. Though she came on another visa, her trafficker brought her to the United States for the purposes of human trafficking because as soon as they arrived in Dallas, the man informed her of the reason that he brought her to the United States. She had no plan to come to the United States prior to meeting her trafficker.

4.  Since her escape, she had been under treatment for Hepatitis C and depression as a result of her experience in the hands of her trafficker. She had no resources to return to the Democratic Republic of Congo and she would not be able to take care of her medical and psychological needs if she was removed.

5.  She complied with a reasonable request for assistance from a law enforcement agency to the extent that ICE was able to conclude that her case was of trafficking in person. She was willing to identify the criminal in video clips and photo lineup.

6. She would suffer extreme hardship involving unusual and severe harm if removed since there was the likelihood of re-victimization in Burundi. She also belongs to a region where there had been civil unrest. The Burundi authorities lack the means or political will to protect her from re-victimization.

## Additional Examples of Human Trafficking Scenarios

### ♦ Victims Used as Factory Workers

Lan and other 250 Vietnamese were held for almost two years while sewing clothing for businesses in American Samoa. More than 90 percent of these "guest workers" were women. They were living under conditions of indentured servitude in crowded rat-infested dormitories. Lan was not paid even the already very low Samoan minimum wage of $2.60 an hour. Instead, she was starved, beaten, sexually harassed, threatened with deportation and imprisonment, while being forced to work for 18 hours a day, seven days a week to fill rush orders.

# ♦ Victim Used as a Domestic Worker

Ami was groomed and promised a wage four-times greater her wage in India before she agreed to be brought to the U.S. to work as a family nanny in New York. She was assured that she would be treated like a family member. However, things changed when Ami arrived. She was coerced to work 15-17 hours a day cleaning, cooking, and doing laundry for the entire family, in addition to the childcare. She had to sleep on the floor while her identity and travel documents were withheld from her by the family. She was threatened with on-the-spot arrest if she went outside without the permission of her employers. She was never paid for the three years of work.

She was thrown out of the family home when she requested permission to attend church alone. She had nowhere to go and no longer had any legal status, so she ended up at a risk of deportation as she had been threatened. A community-based organization whose members spoke Ami's language helped her to locate the police, the FBI, and the DOJ. One of the agencies picked up Ami's case and determined she would be a credible witness in investigating a case of trafficking.

## ♦ Victim Used as a Domestic Servant to Ex-Pat or NIV Holder

Leticia was a domestic servant for a woman whose husband was a US citizen. He was living in the Philippines working for a US company, and his wife was a manager at that company as well. They were very well off, and Leticia liked working for the family. Her wages in the Philippines were good, and she was able to support her elderly mother with what she earned. When Leticia found out the family would relocate to the US temporarily, she was excited to find out they would take her with them. They applied for a B visa for her to come over as a domestic servant during the 6-month period they would be placed in the US. At the consular window, the family had all the papers in order. She remembers doing some things on the computer but doesn't recall having an employment contract, though the law says she should have had to present one to get this type of temporary visa. After a few months in the US, things went sour. The family had overspent their relocation allowance and began taking it out on her. The marriage was suffering, and there were arguments all the time. Leticia would get caught in the middle and would suffer verbal abuse. She felt bad for the kids she was taking care of and kept thinking things would get better. Things only got worse. They cut her wages in half, so that she was not even making minimum wage any more. They would tell her she could not come back with them and her visa would get cancelled at times when they would argue. If she was sick, she still had to work. One time, a wound got infected after she had burned herself cooking for the kids, and they let it fester instead of getting her proper medical attention. The family told her that she should buy groceries for everyone with her wages. They told her they filed to extend her visa, but never gave her any paperwork on that. One day, a neighbor who had helped her with a burn remedy, finally got her to a church for help and the church placed her with a nice family until she could get another job. The family is now back in the Philippines and Leticia is needing help.

## ♦ Victims Used as Restaurant Workers

A man came to Li's village in Korea to recruit young men for jobs in the U.S. He told Li, who was then 16 years old, that he would make enough money to live well and to send home to his family. As Li's parents were getting older and jobs were scarce in the village, Li saw this as an opportunity of a lifetime. With all their savings, his parents paid the man $5,000. Li promised to pay the balance of $20,000 after he arrived.

The man took six other young men along with Li form Korea. The man would give them their travel documents at checkpoints in Korea and Canada and take them back after passing through. The trafficking conditions began when they arrived in Canada as Li was held in captivity for three weeks; he was starved, threatened, and interrogated about his extended family. When Li was brought to the U.S., he was subjected to working 14 hours a day, seven days a week at a Chinese restaurant to settle his arbitrarily growing debt to the traffickers. He was under the close watch of his traffickers and was being threatened with physical harm to his family if he refused to work for even just one day. He was also coerced to perform criminal activities with a threat of harm to his family if he did not agree.

### Victims used as H-2A or H-2B Agricultural or Temporary Workers

Jose came to the US after being sponsored on a valid H-2B visa. He has a contract in Spanish and was recruited by a business in Mexico that is well known for H-2B visas. He did not lie to get his visa – everything was properly filed. When he applied for his visa at the US Consulate, he was even made aware of a human trafficking pamphlet. However, on arrival to the US as a temporary worker, things were not as promised. First, he was made to live in a trailer with many H-2B workers who were responsible for Christmas tree farming in North Carolina. The housing conditions were not as promised, and he wasn't always paid the agreed-on wage, though he did receive regular paychecks. The manager would yell sometimes, saying that he was a slow Mexican and that the "illegals" did better than he did. On rainy days, he would not be paid, and sometimes could only get in 20 hours a week of paid work instead of the 40 hours due to weather conditions. Then he would have to "make it up" by working an 80-hour week the following week, and he felt like he could not make ends meet. The numbers never added up. Finally, he left the Christmas tree farm by just walking away with two other workers, where they eventually were able to call a co-worker's cousin once they got to a nearby gas station. He's been working in cash construction jobs since he left, and now has a great boss. He comes to you with his boss asking if you can get him another H-2B visa to work for that boss, since his wife and kids are in Mexico and this boss wants to "fix" his status by sponsoring him.

## Victims used as L-1B or H-1B IT Consultants

Despite rules against this, Jayesh obtained an H-1B visa through a company that recruited him in India and had him pay for his legal and filing fees by offering him a "training" program. There really wasn't much of a training program, but Jayesh paid $8000 for it because he had heard it was the way to get a sponsor for a visa. He was excited to tell his family that he was coming to the US as an H-1B worker and thought if he did well, he could bring his wife and son, and eventually apply for residency. Jay's job at first was fine. He made the prevailing wage and was at the right job location doing IT consulting work. But then the project ended, and he was "benched" (which is against the H-1B rules). To avoid looking like he was benched, he was supposed to pay $5000 of his hard-earned money under the table to his employer, who could then "funnel" that money into his paychecks so that it would look like he was still getting paid the prevailing wage and still working. This happens several times until Jayesh gets to his breaking point – he is now more in debt than he was when he first came to the US. His wages are high when he is paid, but they disappear fast because when he is not working, he has to "pay" to keep his visa active. Sometimes he works and is not paid for those hours. He comes to you wanting to know if he can transfer his visa and is afraid to turn in his employer because all his friends have a similar problem with the company. He still hasn't been able to get his wife or child to the US, and he is worried they will never get here because he hasn't earned the money to bring them.

## Victims used as J-1 workers

Venkat came to the US as a J-1 worker. Everything was fine, he thought, and it seemed helpful that his J-1 sponsor agency spoke Gujarati and English. A friend in Venkat's town, who really was more of an acquaintance, had introduced him to the program. When Venkat came to Mumbai to board the plane for America, the agent that was helping him wasn't there. Instead it was someone else. That man was named Bipin. Bipin flew with Venkat to the US and helped him get through immigration. Once in the US, Venkat is not given the J-1 job he thought he would have. Instead he is told to work in a laundry. The hours are long, but he is paid normal wages, and he hopes to save up money to travel around America at the end of his program. After six weeks, he is placed with a butcher shop. Venkat cannot do that work because he is a vegetarian Hindu. He is ashamed and Bipin says he will have to take on another job then. Bipin keeps Venkat's passport and charges him money over and over again to "fix" his visa situation, but no new papers ever come. Venkat has not been paid overtime at his newest job, which is working as a box loader at a shipping yard, 16 hours a day. He sleeps in the shipping yard because there is a problem with housing, according to Bipin, and each week he is told it will be one more week. He is college educated and too ashamed to tell his family what has happened. He comes to you after you speak at the Hindu temple one Sunday afternoon, wanting to know if he marries an American, will that help?

## Victims used as sexual servants

Milagro is an undocumented woman who is married with two children. Her undocumented husband has been abusive, but she never reported it. They separated five years ago. When she first came to the US 15 years ago, she was brought in by coyotes. The coyotes raped her repeatedly for over a week while bringing her into the US. She was taken by force and had to do everything they wanted. She doesn't know their names, but remembers some facial features and a distinctive tattoo, and that they talked like they were from Veracruz. Milagro never told her husband what happened because she was so ashamed when the traffickers "delivered" her to her husband in South Carolina, that she felt he would abandon her if she said anything. Finally, she has gotten help from a local Spanish speaking therapist and has started her own embroidery business. Before she left her husband, she used to sew secretly in the night and sell her handiwork to save money to get out of the relationship. She comes to you wanting to know if you can get her a work permit because she owns a small business now. She doesn't understand why you are asking so many questions about what the coyotes did to her.

## Child Victims used as Sexual Servants or in Commercialized Sex

Imelda is a rebellious teenager. She is only 14. She has a pending U-1 and her biological parents each have a derivative U visa pending as a result of the statutory rape case her mother helped initiate against Imelda's boyfriend. Imelda had been taken by a 35-year-old man from South Carolina to North Carolina so that they could live together. Imelda was too young to consent to sex under state law. Imelda is upset that her mother cooperated but after a lot of counseling, seems to understand better why her boyfriend is in jail. Imelda willingly sent him pornographic messages that he sold on the internet when they were dating, and her boyfriend gave her money and gifts whenever she did that. Imelda's mother wants to know if they have to wait 9 years for their U visas, or if there is a faster option for both of them.

## Victims used Construction or Landscaping Workers

Antonio came to the US from Brazil when he was 17 because his earnings were not enough to pay for his mother's medical bills. His father died when he was little. Antonio snuck into the US across the US-Mexico border all by himself – he did not even use a smuggler. Now, Antonio is 35 and has been working in construction for the past 15 years. Before that, he was working in landscaping. His current boss is okay, but he remembers having one construction job where the boss kept saying he would pay him once the general contractor paid the boss. These false promises to pay continued for about 4 months until Antonio finally quit. At the time, Antonio had used all his savings, and kept coming back to work because he really believed he would be paid. When he complained about his paycheck, his boss would "loan" him a few hundred dollars and tell him to "quit bitching, you wetback." His boss would make jokes about Antonio being Mexican all the time, when he knew he was from Brazil, and there are also issues with a lack of safety equipment on the job. When Antonio says he is going to file a wage complaint, his boss stops returning phone calls. Antonio comes to the boss's worksite trailer to ask one last time for his overdue wages, and his boss picks up the phone and says, "get out or I'll call police, and have you deported."

## Victims used as Nail Salon Technicians

Mylin is a nail tech who has been doing nails for the past 2 years at a local salon. She came on a tourist visa and overstayed it. For the first 10 weeks of her job, she was doing "unpaid training." Her boss was okay but said at the end of the 10 weeks she would need to do 6 more weeks of "half-paid" training. Then she started making normal wages. One of the managers at her job is saying that if she doesn't sleep with him, he is going to get her fired. He skims her wages sometimes and says if she complains he will tell the employer she's here illegally. She's been fending him off for a while but is tired of him taking part of her tips and shorting her hours. She wonders if there is a way to extend her expired visa and wishes she could get out of this situation.

## Victims used as Sex Workers

Valeriya came to the US from Russia. She was an F-1 student on scholarship. Unfortunately, she had a sports injury that needed medication. Later she got addicted to pain killers. Eventually she dropped out of school. One of the men who sold her drugs offered to have her pay for those drugs with sex. She was so addicted, she finally gave in. He began "maintaining" her with just enough drugs to keep her from going into withdrawal and had her sell herself to make money to buy more drugs from him. At the worst point in the relationship, her trafficker smacked her around and told her she was a worthless addict before he locked her in the room with a man who had paid to have sex with her. She has one small conviction for prostitution that got deferred under a first-time offender statute. It was after that conviction that she finally got away from her trafficker. She has been on a long road to recovery in recent times and wants to know if her new boyfriend may be able to help her legalize her status through marriage. She is afraid to tell her new boyfriend about her past because her abuser has connections back in Russia that might hurt her parents. Valeriya is worried her past will stop her from immigrating through marriage.

## Victims used as Gas Station Cashiers, Convenient Store Workers, Donut Shop Bakers

Sanjay is a gas station cashier. He used to have a 245i case, or at least, he thought he did. His old boss had filed a labor certification for him for a gas station cashier position on April 29, 2001. Sanjay paid for the legal fees, which were $5000, back when the DOL regulations allowed the foreign national to pay such expenses. Whenever another step needed to be taken in his immigration case, the employer would pretend it was being done, and would not give Sanjay the documentation. Once, Sanjay was told the labor cert was denied on a technicality, so he would have to pay again for the process. Sanjay only talked to a lawyer once and after that, all communication was with the employer only. Sanjay was not paid minimum wage nor overtime by his boss and was told that he would need to manage the store at 60 to 75 hours a week if he wanted to continue to be sponsored for the cashier job. He lived in a small room above the store. After many years of this, Sanjay finally insisted he see the sponsorship paperwork. The employer instead fired him and told him to go to hell and get out or he would call the INS on him. Sanjay was jobless and homeless for a while, and later found a distant relative to live with who helped him get his current job. He is Indian-born, so doing his 245i grandfathered PERM labor cert employment case from scratch might take 12 years or longer. He wants to know if there is another option or if you can find out if his old case was approved so that he can recapture the priority date.

*******

It is likely that most of the victims in the above-listed scenarios would not come to a lawyer's office and begin to tell about what s/he experienced. Instead they may say something like, "I am here illegally, and I want to get a work permit." Or, "I came on a visa but I'm having a problem with it – can you help me?" It is imperative to ask potential clients about the circumstances through which they entered the United States, as well as the conditions that they have had at any employment they have had. Often, they will want to avoid having to tell you what they feel is a most shameful secret. Many will think that if they do not have proof (like a video or police report), that there is nothing they can do now, so they don't want to bother telling you something so painful. Most immigration lawyers do not handle T visas, so it is unlikely that they will have heard about the T visa option or sample scenarios through the immigrant community.

# CHAPTER FOUR

## THE T VISA CONSULTATION PROCESS

Assisting T visa applicants requires that an immigration practitioner understands more than legal implications of trafficking in person. It also calls for a deep understanding of the screening process, application process, how to interact with relevant law enforcement agencies, and how to work with trafficking survivors.

### Ascertain Victims' Immigration Status

As you have seen in the cases analyzed in the preceding chapter, victims of severe forms of trafficking often have issues with their immigration statuses. Many of them are smuggled in without inspection. Some victims enter through a port-of-entry into the United States, but with fraudulent documents (i.e. fake visas, passports, etc.). However, many others enter on a visa. Some enter on visas that do not authorize them to engage in activities that they were involved in. Some, for instance, enter on a B1/B2 tourist visa but wanted to engage in unauthorized employment. They may even overstayed the authorized date on their I-94 Departure Record. Some victims enter the U.S. on valid work visas like as H-2A and H-2B (as temporary agriculture and temporary non-agricultural workers respectively), A-3 and G-5 (domestic employees) but lost their visas because they had to escape from trafficking that their employment turned to. Others may have entered with F-1 visa (for studying) but ended up in the hand of traffickers and lost their statuses.

Though many of these victims fear their lack of immigration status, the Immigration and Nationality Act (INA) 212(a)(9)B(iii) provides that if such victims can prove that trafficking in persons "was at least one central reasons for the alien's unlawful presence in the United States," s/he would not be said to be "unlawfully present." (UP)

At the discretion of USCIS, the victim may be granted a waiver of inadmissibility if s/he applies for such and is otherwise eligible for it. The waiver covers a wide range of inadmissibility.

## Involvement in Criminal Activity

You also need to ascertain the extent of applicant's participation in criminal activity like gunrunning, selling drugs, or prostitution. This is another issue that can come up while considering the applicant for a T status, especially if he was caught in the act, or escaped during the act.

To protect a client from criminal prosecution, you should note that most victims commit these acts involuntarily as the traffickers exercise extreme control over their victims and force them to do their bidding. This should move the attorney to discuss cooperation with the law enforcement agency and arrange how the victim would be protected against criminal or removal proceedings on the basis of his or her statement. The attorney should also consider this in the timing of the T visa application.

Confidentiality and privilege are extremely important in interacting with the client. S/he wants the assurance that the privileged information released during an interview should be not be used against the client and/or out of context.

## Smuggling, Labor Exploitation, and Trafficking

It is imperative to ascertain whether an incident involves solely human smuggling or if the situation turned into human trafficking. Labor exploitation is a part of most trafficking cases however it does not always aggravate to the level of human trafficking. Labor exploitation has to do with working for long hours, in a poor condition with an extremely low wage, without any avenue to seek redress and involves other mistreatments of legal and illegal workers. It can become trafficking when the employer resorts to the use of fraud, force, or coercion to intimidate the victim to prevent him from leaving the situation. Anyone trying to make trafficking claims from exploitation must understand the intricate differences, as well as the federal definition of trafficking.

## Consultation Screening Questions

To determine whether a person has been a victim of human trafficking, you can ask some or all of the following questions during the consultation.

♦ **Migration**

- Who organized your travel to the U.S.?

- Did you enter the United States with a smuggler?

- Who accompanied you?

- How were you brought in?

- Were you informed of this method before your departure?

- Were you in any other countries prior to your arrival to the U.S.?

- Where are the other people that were brought with you?

- Do you know what happened to them?

- Were your travel documents always with you?

- If no, who took them from you?

- Why and how long did they keep them?

- Were you informed of what to say to immigration officials?

- Were you told that if you paid a certain amount of money you would be brought safely to the United States?

## ◆ Arrival

- Where were you put upon arrival?

- What happened to your travel documents and your belongings upon arrival?

- Were you released immediately as promised?

- If not, where were you held?

- What did you have to do there? (cook, clean, etc.)

- How soon were you told to start work?

## ◆ Working Conditions

- What the type of work did you expect to do? (Or did you not expect to work—did you expect to be freed upon arrival?)

- For how many hours were you working per day and how many days per week?

- Were you granted time off?

- Were you allowed to rest if you were sick?

- What was the pay?

- Was it up or close to the amount you agreed to?

- Were the conditions and type of work the same as what you expected or were told?

- Were you living where you worked?

- Could you leave the work or house?

- Were you put in debt bondage or peonage?

- Were you told to work to pay off a loan?

- Do you owe money to your employer, agent, host, or anyone else?

- Were you allowed to communicate with family members?

- With friends or other workers?

- Were you able to attend religious, social, cultural, entertainment, or educational programs?

- ◆ **Recruitment (For those who entered with a work visa)**

   - Who promised to give you the job?

- How much did you agree to be paid and with whom did you agree?

- What were you told about the kind of job or the job condition?

- Was there a signed contract? If yes, where is it?

- What were the terms of the contract?

- Did you or anyone pay someone to bring you to the U.S.?

- What kind of visa or other documents were promised to you?

- Were you sold?

- Were you kidnapped?

## ◆ Domestic Violence

- Did you enter the United States with a significant other?

- Have you ever suffered violence at the hands of an intimate partner?

- Did your partner force you to serve him/ her in any way?

- What did your partner require you to do in the home?

- Did your partner allow you to work?

- Did your partner force you to turn over all your earnings to him/ her?

- Did your partner force you to cook all meals, do all housework, and care for the children without any involvement on his/ her part?

- When you were sick, what were your partner's expectations of you?

- After giving birth, what were your partner's expectations of you?

- Were you allowed to do any activities outside the home other than work?

- Were you forced to have sexual relations against your will?

- Were you ever forced to have sexual relations with other people because your partner required it?

## ♦ Safety and Risk

- Were you threatened with harm at any time?

- Have you experienced...

  - Physical coercion such as:

    - ✓ Threats of violence

- ✓ Physical violence

- ✓ Beatings

- ✓ Torture

- ✓ Sexual harassment

- ✓ Sexual abuse

- ✓ Isolation

- ✓ Imprisonment

- ✓ Incarceration

- ✓ Denial of medical care

- ✓ Denial of food, clothes, or other necessities

- ✓ Others

- Psychological coercion such as:

  - ✓ Deceit

  - ✓ Verbal abuse

  - ✓ Degrading remarks

  - ✓ Abuse of others in front of you

  - ✓ Threats of violence against you or your family, or friends?

  - ✓ Threats to report you to authorities or arrange deportation

- ✓ Speaking in a language you didn't understand

- ✓ Threat of isolation

- ✓ Others

- Do you know the present location or whereabouts of the traffickers?

- Are you presently fearful for your safety or that of anyone else?

- What would happen to you if you were to return home?

These questions can help screen for T Visa eligibility. The initial consultation is not the time to get into every last intimate detail of the case. Once you get a feel for what to look for in human trafficking cases, you will be able to screen for them quickly without forcing the victim to go into too much detail. The large amount of detail should be saved for when the potential client decides to move forward with the case.

# CHAPTER FIVE

## Beginning and Submitting
## a T Visa Case

———————◆———————

The T Visa process is extremely emotional for the victim. You will have to walk the victim step-by-step through circumstances and situations that she or he may not want to think about, let alone speak about. Thus, consideration should be given to the emotional condition of the victim, physical environment of the interview venue, and the use of questions and body languages. It is crucial to have a list of mental health services that you can provide to T Visa clients. Be sure that that list also has an emergency crisis line number.

A trauma-informed interviewing style should be used when working with victims of human trafficking. It is important to be patient and non-judgmental when you meet with the client. Be fully present as a sign of honor to him or her. You must gradually establish a relationship with the client, being sensitive to culture and linguistic differences.

The story may not be sequential at the beginning. It is the duty of the attorney to make a logical and coherent narrative of the events that the client will be bringing out. You can help guide them chronologically as much as possible, however be open to the client telling his or her story out of order. By being fully present and attentive to the client while s/he is explaining what s/he lived through will help you to put the story together in a way that makes sense chronologically. It is important to hear the unsaid and read between the lines, particularly when it comes to the most sensitive parts of the story.

***Physical environment:*** Your office should be prepared in advance to make it comfortable for the client both physically and emotionally. Let your office show that you respect the client. You may use gentle lighting so that you do not have a too bright or too dark office setting that might remind the victim of a past experience. Sitting the clients near the exit door may give him or her an added sense of safety and dispel the fear of feeling trapped.

Be sure to offer water or other drinks throughout the interview. At first the client may refuse a glass of water, but as the interview progresses she or he may become thirsty. Let the client know that you can take a break at any time, and that if they need a moment to step away to the bathroom or step out of the office that they communicate that with you.

**Listen attentively:** You have to be both physically and emotionally present during the meeting. If you give an impression that the client is not your sole focus during the meeting, he may feel that you are not genuinely interested in him or her. Avoid checking emails, using the phone, and typing during the meeting. Let the client know in advance that you are taking notes because you don't want to miss any important information in the case.

**Be supportive of a trauma victim:** Don't forget that you are dealing with a victim of psychological trauma who may be confronting the fact that he is a victim for the very first time in his life. He may not have ever told anyone what he is telling you. You may encounter attitudes like fear, reluctance, anxiety, frustration, anger, difficulty in recalling things, distraction, inconsistencies, and lots more. All of these can be effects of trauma. Do not get nervous, frustrated, or angry. Be supportive and empathetic. Use techniques to help the client through these difficult moments and get back on track with recounting his experience.

***Do not overwhelm the applicant:*** It is understandable that you need have the full understanding of the entire scenario, and in order to do that you have to ask a lot of questions. However, be mindful to not overwhelm the client with too many questions if you see that it is too difficult for her. Do not assume you can get all you need in one meeting. It may take several meetings.

Sometimes the first meeting may be only one hour, and the subsequent meeting(s) can be longer. You may tell the client the aspect of his or her story you would like to focus on during the next meeting as this may help him or her to prepare mentally for the next encounter with you. Some clients want to talk about it all in one meeting, so they can keep moving forward with recovery.

Honor your client's needs. Make an individualized determination of how it is best to proceed for the client.

***Have a list of referrals:*** If you need the services of any social worker or other professional to work on the client, have a list ready and inform the client that you would like him or her to meet with a counselor or anyone rendering the social service appropriate for his or her psychological or physical condition. It is important to always include contact information for a crisis line. Talking about their status as victims of human trafficking is extremely traumatic and painful for some people, and it may require additional mental and physical help.

## Checklist for Assisting a Potential T Nonimmigrant

To be sure you do not miss an important step when a client comes to you or is referred to you, always check the following in the light of all that we have discussed so far:

1. In the first meeting, complete the T1 (and possibly T2, T3, etc.) questionnaire with the client. Begin the T Visa declaration with the T1 applicant. Use the attached declaration questionnaire guide and fill in the answers as you

113

go along. Know that sometimes it takes more than one meeting to be able to complete the declaration questionnaire.

2. In the second meeting, complete the declaration questionnaire if you have not already. If you already have, by the second meeting you should have a complete declaration and completed forms that you review with the client. If the client does not read or speak English, you should be prepared to orally translate the declaration and forms for him or her.

3. Report the case to the Department of Justice, Department of Labor, FBI, and/or any other relevant agencies. Note that a T Visa certification is not required. However, it is ideal to have one. You can request one directly from the agencies to whom you report.

4. Prepare and submit the filing. Be sure to include a fee waiver with your package. A fee waiver is attached here in the addendum.

5. Submit the case to the USCIS and give a copy to the client.

6. Be sure that the client is still in therapy and/or completes a psychological evaluation. Within three months of submitting the case to USCIS, do a follow-up submission where you include the

psychological evaluation and/or therapy notes and/or a letter from the client's therapist.

7. Remain in monthly contact with the client to let him or her know how the case is going.

## Following Up

As soon as you turn in the application with necessary documents with the USCIS, you need to keep track of its status to ensure that it was received and receipted properly, as well as to ensure that you get a biometrics appointment scheduled.

There should be separate receipt notices for forms I-914 (Application for T Non-immigrant Status), I-192 (Waiver), and for an I-765 (Employment Authorization), and any other applications that apply to this case.

It may take between 9 months and a year before a T visa case will be decided (though in 2018, we are seeing about 10.5 months for an approval without an RFE; and with an RFE, add 6 months). If you don't receive any notification of T visa receipt within four weeks, you need to call the T visa unit at (802) 527-4888 and leave a message to have the errors corrected. The same step should be taken if after a year you have not received any message of approval or otherwise of T visa application. You can also email the inquiry to hotlinefollowupi918i914.vsc@uscis. dhs.gov. Attach a G-28, receipts for the pending case, and put the client name and A# and receipt number in email so that USCIS VSC can respond.

# SUMMARY OF THE T VISA PROCESS:

1.  Prepare and Submit the T Visa Application (along with all derivative applications)

2.  Receive the receipts for the T Visa

3.  Receive Biometrics Appointment

4.  If a Request for Evidence is issued by USCIS, prepare and submit the response within the period of time allowed (typically 87 days)

5.  Receive the T Visa Approval

6.  Determine whether T-6 applications or other derivatives must be addressed at this point

7.  If the client is ready to pursue a green card, you may immediately request a letter from the DOJ, DOL, or other LEA stating that the case investigation/prosecution is closed.

8.  If you receive the letter, then immediately apply for permanent residence.

9. If you don't receive the letter, then after 3 years of T status, prepare and submit permanent residence application

10. Receive the permanent residence (a "green card" valid for 10 years)

11. After 5 years, apply for citizenship (naturalization)

# T VISA TOOLKIT!

**This is just the beginning!!! For EVERYTHING you need to know about T Visas, grab our T Visa Toolkit. Inside you will get:**

- Over 20 hours of training on the T Visa (mp3 recordings)

- Over $30,000 worth of work product (redacted motions, T visa applications, templates). We have drawn from many sources in the private and non-profit sector, and put together real world examples of applications and legal briefs, so that you can hit the ground running rather than trying to reinvent the wheel. Even if you have already done some basic T visa cases, this toolkit is a wonderful way to improve your T visa practice.

- "How to" guides on how to handle T Visa RFEs, and sample RFE responses. It is so helpful to see what a 2018

RFE on a T-1 case looks like, so you can proactively try to avoid RFEs (or respond better to the ones you receive)

- Samples of T Visa Appeals and T-visa related motions.

And more!!

Get yours now at:

http://www.amigalawyers.com/services/tvisa

The T Visa Toolkit/Seminar Purchase link allows you to order online. A flash drive with over 180 items on it, including the mp3 recordings, sample T filings, templates, sample motions and briefs related to T visa cases, and reference materials, will be mailed to you upon receiving your order. This toolkit is designed so that you can see what a proper T visa filing is like, and so that you can review and modify briefs and templates for your own use at the law office for your T visa clients. It is not just a starter kit – it is comprehensive.

# APPENDIX

To obtain all of the documents in the Appendix online,

please visit www.Tvisa.info .

# APPENDIX A:

———◇———

## T Visa Declaration Guidance Questionnaire (For general trafficking cases as well as smuggling turned trafficking)

Declaration Notes for: Click here to enter text          .

What are the circumstances of your entry into the United States?

Click here to enter text.

What was the purpose for which you were brought to the United States?

Click here to enter text.

When did things begin to change or appear different from what you originally thought would happen?

## FORCE

Did anyone use weapons against you?

Click here to enter text.

Did anyone threaten you with weapons?

Click here to enter text.

Did anyone use weapons against others in your presence?

Click here to enter text.

Did you witness anyone else having weapons used against them?

Click here to enter text.

Did anyone touch you in a way that was offensive to you? Such as grabbing you by the arm, pulling you by the hair, grabbing you by the ear, pinching you, pulling you by the leg or foot?

Click here to enter text.

Did you see anyone touched in such a way?

Click here to enter text.

Did anyone touch you in an intimate way, such as fondling your breasts or genitalia? (This question is for men and women)

Click here to enter text.

Did they ever threaten you with rape?

Click here to enter text.

Did they ever rape you?

Click here to enter text.

Did they ever threaten to rape your child and/or wife?

Click here to enter text.

Did they ever rape your child and/or wife?

Click here to enter text.

Were you ever physically restrained? If so, how?

Click here to enter text.

Were you ever forced into an area and unable to move or leave?

Click here to enter text.

Were you ever locked in a room?

Click here to enter text.

Were you ever held in isolation for a long period of time?

Click here to enter text.

## Fraud

Did they make promises to you that they did not keep? What were the promises that they made to you?

Click here to enter text.

Did they tell you that they could offer you a better life somehow?

Click here to enter text.

Did they guarantee you that you would arrive to the United States safely?

Click here to enter text.

Did they promise you legal status in the United States?

Click here to enter text.

Did they try to create romantic relationship with you to try to have you do what s/he wanted?

Click here to enter text.

Did they promise you a job opportunity that did not actually exist?

Click here to enter text.

Did they promise you a job but provided you with a different job?

Click here to enter text.

Did they misrepresent your salary or working hours in a job that they said they would provide to you?

Click here to enter text.

Did they misrepresent the living conditions or make fake promises about the living conditions?

Click here to enter text.

## Coercion

Did they threaten to harm you?

Click here to enter text.

Did they actually harm you?

Click here to enter text.

Did they threaten to restrain you in some way, such as holding you in a room, house, apartment or some other place where you could not leave?

Click here to enter text.

Did they threaten to physically restrain you? Such as tie you up, put on handcuffs, cover your mouth with tape or a gag?

Click here to enter text.

Did they tell you that if you did a certain act, then you or another person would be harmed? For example, if you tried to escape, if you tried to tell the police, if you tried to resist them, etc.

Did they tell you that if you failed to do a certain act then you or another person would be harmed? For example, if you did not pay additional money, if you did not work for them, if you did not have sex with them, if you did not use drugs with them, etc.

Click here to enter text.

Did they threaten to turn you over to immigration if you escaped or failed to comply with their demands?

Click here to enter text.

Did they threaten to have you deported if you did not do what they said?

Click here to enter text.

Did they threaten to harm your family?

Click here to enter text.

Did they threaten your family? Who did they threaten?

Click here to enter text.

Did you believe that they could and/or would follow through with those threats?

Click here to enter text.

Did they start a romantic relationship with you that they used for their own benefit, such as to make you serve them, have sex with them or others on demand, etc.?

Click here to enter text.

Did they use your poverty or desperation against you?

Click here to enter text.

Did they withhold your travel documents or other identity documents such as passports, visas, etc.?

*Click here to enter text.*

Did they create a situation that forced you to become undocumented, such as allowing your visa to expire?

*Click here to enter text.*

Did they socially isolate you?

*Click here to enter text.*

Did they limit your interaction with your family or anyone else that you knew?

*Click here to enter text.*

Were you constantly being watched by them? Was there ever a moment where you were unsupervised by them?

*Click here to enter text.*

Did they demand that you do work in dangerous or difficult conditions?

*Click here to enter text.*

Did they demand that you work unreasonably long hours?

*Click here to enter text.*

Did they say that you owed an additional debt that you had to work off with them?

Click here to enter text.

Were you forced to turn over your paychecks or did payments by your employer "bounce" or get cancelled?

Click here to enter text.

Did they force you to use drugs or other substances against your will?

Click here to enter text.

Did they create a drug problem in you because of forcing you to use and be exposed to drugs?

Click here to enter text.

Did they shame you? For what?

Click here to enter text.

Did they use the fact that you don't speak English against you?

Click here to enter text.

Did they restrict your access to food and necessities so that you were dependent on them?

Click here to enter text.

Did they restrict, delay, or withhold access to medical care?

Click here to enter text.

Did they deny you the opportunity to go to school?

Click here to enter text.

Did they intimidate you by showing you that there were a lot of people involved in the group? For example, so that you didn't think you could escape or didn't know who you could trust.

Click here to enter text.

Did they cause you financial harm? Did they steal from you? Take away any financial means of independence? Did they refuse to pay you, or did they continue to make you work with false promises to pay you? Did checks you were supposed to receive for payment, bounce? (i.e. be rejected for insufficient funds)

Click here to enter text.

Did they confuse you with their words and actions? Such as by telling you one thing and then telling you the complete opposite, or doing one thing and then denying that they did it, or saying one thing and doing something different?

Click here to enter text.

Did they wear down your energy so that you were physically and/or mentally unable or unwilling to escape?

Click here to enter text.

## Escape from Traffickers

How and when did you escape, were rescued, or otherwise became separated from the traffickers?

Click here to enter text.

Have you had contact with your traffickers since they escaped?

Click here to enter text.

Have your traffickers contacted your family since you escaped?

Click here to enter text.

Do you fear your traffickers?

Click here to enter text.

What do you think that they would do if they found you?

Click here to enter text.

## Life After Trafficking

What have you been doing since you were separated from the traffickers?

Click here to enter text.

Why were you unable to leave the United States after you were separated from the traffickers?

Click here to enter text.

How has this experience affected you?

What harm or mistreatment do you fear if you are removed from the United States?

Click here to enter text.

Why do you fear you would be harmed or mistreated?

Click here to enter text.

What are your hopes and dreams for the Future?

Click here to enter text.

# APPENDIX B:

## Wage and Hour Theft Declaration Questionnaire

Declaration Notes for: Click here to enter text          .

What are the circumstances of your entry into the United States?

Click here to enter text.

When you hired a coyote, what were the terms? How much was it going to cost? What did they promise (a quick passing, not a lot of walking, etc, etc)? When did you have to pay? Where were they going to take you inside the US?

Click here to enter text.

When did things begin to change or appear different from what you originally thought would happen?

Click here to enter text.

## Employment

What were the terms of your employment? Were you going to be paid hourly or a set amount? What was the amount? How often were you going to be paid? (every 15 days, once a month, etc) Were you paid a salary? Who controlled your tasks at work?

Click here to enter text.

Were you going to be an employee or an independent contractor? If independent contractor, did you receive a contract? Do you have a copy of the contract? If IC, do you have your own business?

Click here to enter text.

How did you keep track of your hours? Were you able to clock in and clock out? Was there a formal way to report your hours? Were records (either paper or electronic) kept? Were you given an opportunity to sign your time sheets?

Click here to enter text.

Did your employer pay you less than what you were owed? If yes, why do you believe this?

Click here to enter text.

Were you ever threatened that they would call immigration against you?

Click here to enter text.

Were you ever verbally threatened at your work?

Click here to enter text.

Did they ever yell at you? Call you names?

Click here to enter text.

Were you ever physically harmed at your work? Such as pushing, punching, hitting, slapping, sexual assault, etc?

Click here to enter text.

Were you ever provided with safety training? Safety equipment?

Click here to enter text.

Were there posters up about employee rights and employer responsibilities?

Click here to enter text.

Did you ever complain about not being paid? When? To who?

Click here to enter text.

What was your work schedule?

Click here to enter text.

Were you given a time to eat lunch?

Click here to enter text.

Were you given breaks throughout the day?

Click here to enter text.

Why didn't you return to your country?

Click here to enter text.

What would you do if you had to return to your country today? (not just that you don't *want* to go—but if you were physically there, what would you do?) Where would you live?

Click here to enter text.

Who in your family lives in your home country? Would you be able to stay with them?

Click here to enter text.

Would you be able to get a job?

Click here to enter text.

**Life After Trafficking**

What have you been doing since you were separated from the traffickers?

Click here to enter text.

Why were you unable to leave the United States after you were separated from the traffickers?

Click here to enter text.

How has this experience affected you?

What harm or mistreatment do you fear if you are removed from the United States?

Click here to enter text.

Why do you fear you would be harmed or mistreated?

Click here to enter text.

What are your hopes and dreams for the Future?

Click here to enter text.

# APPENDIX C

---

## Domestic Violence-Based Trafficking

### T Visa Domestic Violence Questions

### Fraud:

Did your partner promise you a better life if you came to the US with them? (or were you already in an abusive relationship and felt you had no choice but to enter the US with your partner?)

Click or tap here to enter text.

### Force/Coercion:

Did your partner threaten to harm you/your family or actually harm you?

Click or tap here to enter text.

Did your partner use violence to make you feel like you had no choice but to do whatever they demanded?

Click or tap here to enter text.

Did your partner want to know where you were at all times?

Click or tap here to enter text.

Did your partner isolate you and prevent you from talking to your friends and family?

Click or tap here to enter text.

Did your partner threaten to have you deported or arrested, or to call immigration, if you didn't do what he said in addition to using violence against you?

Click or tap here to enter text.

Did your partner take your passport or identity documents?

Click or tap here to enter text.

Did they restrict your movement or ever lock you in a room?

Click or tap here to enter text.

## Labor Trafficking:

Please describe some expectations that your abuser/ex partner had regarding housework. (ie specific meals to be provided at specific times, or instructions on cleaning, or other expectations?

Click or tap here to enter text.

Can you tell me how your partner would react when housework wasn't done according to his instructions? What did they say to you and what would they do? (giving 2 or 3 specific examples with approximate dates is helpful)

Click or tap here to enter text.

Did your partner expect you to babysit or otherwise care for/do housework for other family members, like stepchildren, in-laws, etc.? If so, how often and what exactly?

Click or tap here to enter text.

What was your daily routine in terms of housework?

Click or tap here to enter text.

Did your partner allow you to have breaks from housework, like if you were sick or during your pregnancy?

Click or tap here to enter text.

Did your partner ever arrange work for you outside of the home and take the money you earned for themselves?

Click or tap here to enter text.

Did your partner expect you/force you to pay his bills or the rent with the money you earned?

Click or tap here to enter text.

Did your partner ever tell you that you owed him money, or had a debt to pay off? If so, how did he suggest that you would pay this debt off and how much did you "owe" him, or did that amount continue to change over time?

Click or tap here to enter text.

## Sexual Servitude

Did your partner expect you or force you to have sexual relations with them whenever they wanted to?

Click or tap here to enter text.

## Living Conditions

Did your partner withhold money from you so that you always had to ask them if you needed something?

Click or tap here to enter text.

Did you have access to enough food?

Click or tap here to enter text.

Did your partner restrict your access to medical attention?

Click or tap here to enter text.

## Reporting to Law Enforcement

Did you ever report your partner to the police or any other member of law enforcement? Where and what happened?

Click or tap here to enter text.

## Extreme Hardship Upon Removal

Does your partner know where your family members are in your country of origin and have they made threats against them?

Click or tap here to enter text.

Do you feel they would find you or harm you, or send someone to harm you if you were forced to return to your country?

Click or tap here to enter text.

What other fears do you have about returning to your country?

Click or tap here to enter text.

Did you ever go to therapy in the US to talk about your experience?

Click or tap here to enter text.

What are you hopes and dreams for the future in the United States?

Click or tap here to enter text.

# APPENDIX D:

---

## T-1 Form Questionnaire

Interpreter: ☐ Yes ☐ No

First Name: Click here to enter text .

Last Name: Click here to enter text .

Middle Name: Click here to enter text .

Other Names Used: Click here to enter text.A#: Click here to enter text

Social Security #: Click here to enter text.Gender:

☐Male

☐Female

Marital Status:

☐ Single

☐ Married

☐ Divorced

☐ Widowed:

DOB: Click here to enter a date.

Country of Birth /Citizenship: Click here to enter text.

City of Birth: Click here to enter text.

State of Birth: Click here to enter text.Passport #: Enter text.

Issuance: Enter text.

Date Issued: Enter text.

Place of Last Entry: Click here to enter text.

Date of Last Entry: Enter date.

Previous of Entries: (Date [From -To], Place, Status):

Click here to enter text.

Click here to enter text.

Mother's Name: Click here to enter text.

DOB: Click here to enter text.

City/ Country of Birth: Click here to enter text.

Current City/ Country:Click here to enter text.

Father's Name: Click here to enter text.

DOB: Click here to enter text.

City/ Country of Birth:Click here to enter text.

Current City/ Country:Click here to enter text.

☐ **Spouse:**

Last Name: Click here to enter text.

First Name: Click here to enter text.

Middle Name: Click here to enter text.

DOB: Click here to enter a date.

Country of Birth: Click here to enter text.

Current Location: Click here to enter text.

☐ **Children:**

Last Name: Click here to enter text.

First Name: Click here to enter text.

Middle Name: Click here to enter text.

DOB: Click here to enter a date.

Relationship: Click here to enter text.

Country of Birth: Click here to enter text.

Current Location: Click here to enter text.

Last Name: Click here to enter text.

First Name: Click here to enter text.

Middle Name: Click here to enter text.

DOB: Click here to enter a date.

Relationship: Click here to enter text.

Country of Birth: Click here to enter text.

Current Location: Click here to enter text.

Last Name: Click here to enter text.

First Name: Click here to enter text.

Middle Name: Click here to enter text.

DOB: Click here to enter a date.

Relationship: Click here to enter text.

Country of Birth: Click here to enter text.

Current Location:Click here to enter text.

Last Name: Click here to enter text.

First Name: Click here to enter text.

Middle Name: Click here to enter text.

DOB: Click here to enter a date.

Relationship: Click here to enter text.

Country of Birth: Click here to enter text.

Current Location:Click here to enter text.

Last Name: Click here to enter text.

First Name: Click here to enter text.

Middle Name: Click here to enter text.

DOB: Click here to enter a date.

Relationship: Click here to enter text.

Country of Birth: Click here to enter text.

Current Location:Click here to enter text.

## Residence (Past 5 Years):

| Address | City | State | From | To |
|---------|------|-------|------|-----|
| Click here to enter text. | Click here to enter text. | Click here to enter text. | Text here. | Text here |
| Click here to enter text. | Click here to enter text. | Click here to enter text. | Text here. | Text here |
| Click here to enter text. | Click here to enter text. | Click here to enter text. | Text here. | Text here |
| Click here to enter text. | Click here to enter text. | Click here to enter text. | Text here. | Text here |
| Click here to enter text. | Click here to enter text. | Click here to enter text. | Text here. | Text here |

## Biographical Information:

Ethnicity: ☐ Hispanic/Latino ☐ Not Hispanic/Latino

Race: ☐ White ☐ Asian ☐ Black/African American ☐ American Indian ☐ American Indian/Alaska Native ☐ Native Hawaiian/Other Pacific Islander

Height: Ft and In _____

Weight: lbs _____

Eye Color: Color

Hair Color: Color

Have you previously filed an application for advance permission to enter the US as a nonimmigrant?

☐Yes

☐No

Have you ever applied for employment authorization?

☐Yes

☐No

Committed a crime or offense for which you have not been arrested?

☐Yes

☐No

Been arrested, cited, or detained by any law enforcement officer (including DHS, former INS, and military officers) for any reason?

☐Yes

☐No

Been charged with committing any crime or offense?

☐Yes

☐No

Been convicted of a crime or offense (even if violation was subsequently expunged or pardoned)?

☐Yes

☐No

Been placed in an alternative sentencing or a rehabilitative program (for example: diversion, deferred prosecution, withheld adjudication, deferred adjudication)?

☐Yes

☐No

Received a suspended sentence, been placed on probation, or been paroled?

☐Yes

☐No

Been in jail or prison?

☐Yes

☐No

Been the beneficiary of a pardon, amnesty, rehabilitation, or other act of clemency or similar action?

☐Yes

☐No

Exercised diplomatic immunity to avoid prosecution for a criminal offense in the United States?

☐Yes

☐No

| Crime | Date of incident | City, State, Country | Outcome |
|---|---|---|---|
| Click here to enter text. | Click here to enter text. | Click here to enter text. | Click here to enter text. |
| Click here to enter text. | Click here to enter text. | Click here to enter text. | Click here to enter text. |

| Click here to enter text. | Click here to enter text. | Click here to enter text. | Click here to enter text. |
|---|---|---|---|
| Click here to enter text. | Click here to enter text. | Click here to enter text. | Click here to enter text. |

## Additional Notes

Engaged in prostitution or procurement of prostitution or do you intend to engage in prostitution or procurement of prostitution?

☐Yes

☐No

EVER engaged in any unlawful commercialized vice, including, but not limited to illegal gambling?

☐Yes

☐No

EVER knowingly encouraged, induced, assisted, abetted, or aided any alien to try to enter the United States illegally?

☐Yes

☐No

EVER illicitly trafficked in any controlled substance, or knowingly assisted, abetted, or colluded in the illicit trafficking of any controlled substance?

☐Yes

☐No

Have you EVER committed, planned or prepared, participated in, threatened to, attempted to, or conspired to commit, gathered information for, or solicited funds for any of the following:

Hijacking or sabotage of any conveyance (including an aircraft, vessel, or vehicle)?

☐Yes

☐No

Seizing or detaining, and threatening to kill, injure, or continue to detain, another individual in order to compel a third person (including a governmental organization) to do or abstain from doing any act as an explicit or implicit condition for the release of the individual seized or detained?

☐Yes

☐No

Assassination?

☐Yes

☐No

The use of any firearm with intent to endanger, directly or indirectly, the safety of one or more individual or to cause substantial damage to property?

☐Yes

☐No

The use of any biological agent; chemical agent; or nuclear weapon or device; explosive; or other weapon or dangerous device, with intent to endanger, directly or indirectly, the safety of one or more individuals or to cause substantial damage to property?

☐Yes

☐No

Have you EVER been a member of, solicited money or members for, provided support for, attended military training (as defined in section 2339D(c)(1) of title 18, United States Code) by or on behalf of, or been associated with an organization that is:

Designated as a terrorist organization under section 219 of the Immigration and Nationality Act?

☐Yes

☐No

Any other group of two or more individuals, whether organized or not, which has engaged in or has a subgroup which has engaged in:

Hijacking or sabotage of any conveyance (including an aircraft, vessel, or vehicle)?

☐Yes

☐No

Seizing or detaining, and threatening to kill, injure, or continue to detain another individual in order to compel a third person (including a governmental organization) to do or abstain from doing any act as an explicit or implicit condition for the release of the individual seized or detained?

☐Yes

☐No

Assassination?

☐Yes

☐No

The use of any firearm with intent to endanger, directly or indirectly, the safety of one or more individual or to cause substantial damage to property?

☐Yes

☐No

Soliciting money or members or otherwise providing material support to a terrorist organization?

☐Yes

☐No

The use of any biological agent; chemical agent; or nuclear weapon or device; explosive, or other weapon or dangerous device, with intent to endanger, directly or indirectly, the safety of one or more individuals or to cause substantial damage to property?

☐Yes

☐No

Do you intend to engage in the United States in:

Espionage?

☐Yes

☐No

Any unlawful activity, or any activity the purpose of which is in opposition, to control, or overthrow of the government of the United States?

☐Yes

☐No

Solely, principally, or incidentally in any activity related to espionage or sabotage or to violate any law involving the export of goods, technology, or sensitive information?

☐Yes

☐No

Have you ever been or do you continue to be a member of the Communist or other totalitarian party, except when membership was involuntary?

☐Yes

☐No

Have you, during the period of March 23, 1933, to May 8, 1945, in association with either the Nazi Government of Germany or any organization or government associated or allied with the Nazi Government of Germany, ever ordered, incited, assisted, or otherwise participated in the persecution of any person because of race, religion, nationality, membership in a particular social group, or political opinion?

☐Yes

☐No

Have you EVER been present or nearby when any person was:

Intentionally killed, tortured, beaten, or injured?

☐Yes

☐No

Displaced or moved from his or her residence by force, compulsion, or duress?

☐Yes

☐No

In any way compelled or forced to engage in any kind of sexual contact or relations?

☐Yes

☐No

Are removal, exclusion, rescission, or deportation proceedings pending against you?

☐Yes

☐No

Have removal, exclusion, rescission, or deportation proceedings EVER been initiated against you?

☐Yes

☐No

Have you EVER been removed, excluded, or deported from the United States?

☐Yes

☐No

Have you EVER been ordered to be removed, excluded, or deported from the United States?

☐Yes

☐No

Have you EVER been denied a visa or denied admission to the United States? (If a visa was denied, explain why on a separate sheet of paper.)

☐Yes

☐No

Have you EVER been granted voluntary departure by an immigration officer or an immigration judge and failed to depart within the allotted time?

☐Yes

☐No

Have you EVER ordered, incited, called for, committed, assisted, helped with, or otherwise participated in any of the following:

Acts involving torture or genocide?

☐Yes

☐No

Killing any person?

☐Yes

☐No

Intentionally and severely injuring any person?

☐Yes

☐No

Engaging in any kind of sexual contact or relations with any person who was being forced or threatened?

☐Yes

☐No

Limiting or denying any person's ability to exercise religious beliefs?

☐Yes

☐No

Have you EVER:

Served in, been a member of, assisted in, or participated in any military unit, paramilitary unit, police unit, self-defense unit, vigilante unit, rebel group, guerrilla group, militia, or insurgent organization?

☐Yes

☐No

Served in any prison, jail, prison camp, detention facility, labor camp, or any other situation that involved detaining persons?

☐Yes

☐No

Have you EVER been a member of, assisted in, or participated in any group, unit, or organization of any kind in which you or other persons used any type of weapon against any person or threatened to do so?

☐Yes

☐No

Have you EVER assisted or participated in selling or providing weapons to any person who to your knowledge used them against another person, or in transporting weapons to any person who to your knowledge used them against another person?

☐Yes

☐No

Have you EVER received any type of military, paramilitary, or weapons training?

☐Yes

☐No

Are you under a final order or civil penalty for violating section 274C (producing and/or using false documentation to unlawfully satisfy a requirement of the Immigration and Nationality Act)?

☐Yes

☐No

Have you EVER, by fraud or willful misrepresentation of a material fact, sought to procure, or procured, visa or other documentation, for entry into the United States or any immigration benefit?

☐Yes

☐No

Have you EVER left the United States to avoid being drafted into the U.S. Armed Forces?

☐Yes

☐No

Have you EVER been a J nonimmigrant exchange visitor who was subject to the two-year foreign residence requirement and not yet complied with that requirement or obtained a waiver of such?

☐Yes

☐No

Have you EVER detained, retained, or withheld the custody of a child, having a lawful claim to U.S. citizenship, outside the United States from a U.S. citizen granted custody?

☐Yes

☐No

Do you plan to practice polygamy in the United States?

☐Yes

☐No

Have you entered the United States as a stowaway?

☐Yes

☐No

Do you have a communicable disease of public health significance?

☐Yes

☐No

Do you have or have you had a physical or mental disorder and behavior (or a history of behavior that is likely to recur) associated with the disorder which has posed or may pose a threat to the property, safety, or welfare of yourself or others?

☐Yes

☐No

Are you now or have you been a drug abuser or drug addict?

☐Yes

☐No

# APPENDIX E:

## Fee Waiver

### REQUEST FOR FEE WAIVER

CURRENT TOTAL DEBT:         $Amount

Current Monthly Expenses:

Mortgage Payment:         $Amount

Car Insurance:         $Amount

Car Payments:         $Amount

Medical Insurance:         $Amount

Water & Sewer & Garbage:         $Amount

Cable:         $Amount

Light         $Amount

| | |
|---|---|
| Gas | $Amount |
| Bus: | $Amount |
| Groceries: | $Amount |
| Cell Phones: | $Amount |
| Daycare ___ days a week: | $Amount |
| <u>Total Monthly Expenses:</u> | $Amount |

With my income of Amount each month, I have very little left over for living expenses and any sort of "extras" for my family. Paying a filing fee would be very difficult for me. For this reason, I respectfully request that the fee be waived in this matter.

*If applicable: I do not receive paychecks because _____ and as a result I do not have any W-2s for the most recent tax year. [describe evidence attached related to budget and income and expenses; describe any dependent family members and include documentation of such dependents; and if the client is married to the abuser, be sure to note that here so that the abuser's income documents won't be requested. Please see USCIS fee waiver guidance and form instructions for I-*

*912 form for further information on preparing a detailed fee waiver request.*

Sincerely,

Client Name

# APPENDIX F:

## Sample T Visa Cover Letter

Date :

VIA FEDERAL EXPRESS

T Visa Unit

U.S. Citizenship & Immigration Services

Vermont Service Center

75 Lower Weldon St

St Albans, VT 05479-0001

## RE: Petition for T Nonimmigrant Status (I-914) and I-192 Waiver

**Applicant: Name DOB Date**

Dear Sir or Madam:

_____ is representing Name
("First Name"). A signed form G-28 is enclosed. Name
is applying for a T visa as s/he has been a victim of a
severe form of trafficking in persons and because s/he
would face extreme hardship involving severe and
unusual harm if the U.S. removed to Country. Name is
willing to cooperate in any way with an investigation
into the case against the trafficker.

Name is eligible for T Nonimmigrant Status. To be
eligible for such status, the applicant must show that: (1)
they have been a victim of a severe form of trafficking in
persons; (2) is physically present in the United States as
a result of trafficking; (3) has complied with any
reasonable request for assistance in the investigation
and prosecution of acts of trafficking in persons; and (4)
would suffer extreme hardship involving severe and
unusual harm upon removal. *See* Filing Instructions for
Form I-914, Section 3; 8 U.S.C.A. § 1101(a)(15)(T); 8
C.F.R. § 214.11.

Summary of trafficking

Additionally, Trafficker created and fostered an environment of intimidation and fear that further limited Name's ability to assert his/her rights or realize the promises made to him/her. Summary of conditions of fear

## 1. Name **is a victim of a severe form of trafficking in persons:**

Name is a victim of human trafficking in persons, which has been defined as "the recruitment, harboring, transportation, provision, or obtaining of a person for labor or services, through the use of force, fraud, or coercion for the purpose of subjection to involuntary servitude, peonage, debt bondage, or slavery." 22 U.S.C.A. §7102 (8)(B).

Name was trafficked for _____ (fill in with labor or services) by the use of:

Force:

- Bullet point here the force that was used

Fraud:

- Bullet point here the fraud that was used

Coercion:

- Bullet point here the coercion that was used

S/he was subjected into _____
(fill in either involuntary servitude, peonage, debt bondage, or slavery; if it's multiple, list all).

- Give examples bullet pointed here to show how it meets this.

## 2. Name **is physically present in the United States as a result of trafficking:**

Name was brought to the United States by a human trafficker. The details are outlined in Name's declaration.

## 3. Name **is willing to report the trafficking and comply with reasonable requests for assistance in the investigation and prosecution of acts of trafficking in persons:**

Despite Name's fears, Name remains willing to assist in the investigation of the trafficker in order to ensure that no other persons are tricked into coming to the U.S. through false promises and then trapped with no means to return home.

4. Name **would suffer extreme hardship involving severe and unusual harm upon removal to the** Country:

Name is extremely vulnerable to being subjected to trafficking in persons again. Unemployment, underemployment and poverty are severe problems in Country.

Additionally, as the case is investigated, Name needs to stay in the United States to assist in the investigation of the trafficking violation committed by the trafficker. If Name leaves, the investigators will not have the benefit of Name's cooperation. Name intends to remain available as a witness and to assist in the investigation of this case.

## 5. Name **is deserving of discretion for the T Visa and waiver**

Name has the "usual" immigration violations of illegal entry to the United States, unlawful presence, unlawful employment, and working with false documents. However, Name has paid His/her taxes every single year, which is a presumptive good moral character factor. S/he strives to be contributing member of society.

For the reasons listed above and those that may be found within this application, we respectfully request that Name be granted a T-Visa.

Sincerely,




ATTORNEY

# APPENDIX G:

---

## Sample Detailed T Visa Cover Letter for Human Smuggling Turned Human Trafficking

**RE: Petition for T Nonimmigrant Status (I-914) and I-192 Waiver**

**Applicant: Name DOB Date**

Dear Sir or Madam:

Our office is representing Name ("First Name"). A signed form G-28 is enclosed. Name is applying for a T visa as s/he has been a victim of a severe form of trafficking in persons and because s/he would face extreme hardship involving severe and unusual harm if the U.S. removed to Country. Name is willing to cooperate in any way with an investigation into the case against the trafficker.

Name is eligible for T Nonimmigrant Status. To be eligible for such status, the applicant must show that: (1) they have been a victim of a severe form of trafficking in persons; (2) is physically present in the United States as a result of trafficking; (3) has complied with any reasonable request for assistance in the investigation and prosecution of acts of trafficking in persons; and (4) would suffer extreme hardship involving severe and unusual harm upon removal. *See* Filing Instructions for Form I-914, Section 3; 8 U.S.C.A. § 1101(a)(15)(T); 8 C.F.R. § 214.11.

Summary of trafficking

Additionally, Trafficker created and fostered an environment of intimidation and fear that further limited Name's ability to assert his/her rights or realize the promises made to him/her. Summary of conditions of fear

## 6. Name **is a victim of a severe form of trafficking in persons:**

Name is a victim of human trafficking in persons, which has been defined as "the recruitment, harboring, transportation, provision, or obtaining of a person for labor or services, through the use of force, fraud, or coercion for the purpose of subjection to involuntary servitude, peonage, debt bondage, or slavery." 22 U.S.C.A. §7102 (8)(B).

**The traffickers harbored, transported, provided and obtained** Name **for labor and services in the United States.**

- The coyote-trafficker who met the applicant near the border in Mexico and helped him/her cross the U.S./Mexico border effectively transported him/her and exploited him/her for domestic labor and involuntary servitude.

- The trafficker harbored the applicant by housing him/her in their home, preventing him/her from leaving, and keeping him/her isolated in the house, while benefiting from his/her labor.

**The traffickers used *force, fraud, and coercion* to harbor, transport, provide and obtain** Name **to provide domestic labor and services.**

Force:

- By physically restraining Name from leaving the home or escaping, locking him/her in the house and maintaining him/her under constant supervision, and threatening him/her with physical harm, the traffickers used <u>force</u> to obtain Name's labor.

Fraud:

- The original coyote-trafficker used <u>fraud</u> to transport and provide Name for labor by deceiving Name about the conditions of the arrangement to be taken across the U.S./Mexico border and about the ultimate purpose for Name after crossing the border. The situation created by the traffickers differed significantly from what they promised Name, which was safe passage to the United States, and the deception enabled unjust gain Name's labor.

Coercion:

- Through constant pressure and monitoring, isolation, lack of contact with family or outsiders, insufficient access to food, threats of harm and deportation, denial of access to phones or transportation, and emotional abuse, the traffickers used <u>coercion</u> to obtain Name's labor and maintain His/her in involuntary servitude.

The traffickers' collective <u>coercive, fraudulent and forceful</u> actions, mistreatment and abuse caused Name fear and physically restrained him/her so that s/he believed that if s/he tried to escape—if s/he did not continue providing forced domestic labor for the traffickers—s/he would suffer serious harm.

**The traffickers harbored, transported, provided and obtained the applicant for** *the purposes of involuntary servitude.*

- The traffickers' plan to transport, harbor, provide and obtain Name for labor/involuntary servitude began in Mexico when the original coyote-trafficker offered him/her the opportunity to be transported to the United States, across the border. They capitalized on the poor economic situation and desire to migrate to the United States and escape him/her situation in Mexico, attracting him/her with a simple (yet fraudulent) offer of safe passage to the United States.

- The fraudulent offer of safe passage was sufficient to obtain Name's initial acquiescence, since Name was looking for assistance to enter the United States.

- The original coyote-trafficker was able to provide Name to the traffickers in the United States, because Name did not know what awaited across the border. By the time Name was in the custody of the coyote-trafficker, s/he was effectively trapped, unable to get out of the situation.

- The traffickers specifically selected Name, noting that s/he who was traveling alone and had virtually no protection or support that would enable Name to prevent or escape the involuntary servitude.

- The traffickers in the United States, were able to maintain Name in involuntary servitude because they kept him/her isolated, scared and trapped. They prohibited him/her from even stepping outside the house or standing close to the windows. The house was locked with keys and Name was under constant supervision, prohibited from even speaking to the others trapped there with him/her. The traffickers also denied him/her access to sufficient food and hygiene and repeatedly threatened him/her with harm. These actions prevented him/her escape and caused him/her to fear harm if attempting to escape.

- While keeping him/her locked in the house, the traffickers exploited Name's vulnerabilities to force him/her to provide domestic labor for them, which constitutes involuntary servitude.

- The traffickers' actions caused Name to fear that him/her would suffer harm—whether physical, economic, psychological or otherwise—if him/her did not continue to provide the labor they demanded.

**The evidence shows that _____ 's case is a situation of smuggling turned trafficking, not simply smuggling.**

- Alien smuggling involves an arrangement made with a smuggler to enter the United States illegally; in contrast, human trafficking involves the use of force, fraud and/or coercion to subject someone to involuntary servitude.

- A situation that begins as human smuggling can turn into human trafficking if the

182

smuggler/trafficker uses force, fraud or coercion to subject the alien to involuntary servitude.

- The facts show that Name was exploited after the journey to the United States for labor instead of simply receiving safe passage in exchange for an agreed-upon payment. The facts show that the original coyote-trafficker did not part ways with Name after bringing him/her into the United States as happens in smuggling situations.

- The facts show that Name was coerced and forced to provide labor to the traffickers for several weeks, which distinguishes him/her situation from simple smuggling.

**_____'s case is analogous to other cases where U.S. courts found defendants criminally or civilly liable for trafficking, involuntary servitude and/or forced labor.**

- In *U.S. v. Soto et al*, a U.S. district court found several defendants guilty of involuntary servitude and other related charges.

- In *U.S. v. Leon-Aldana*, a U.S. district court indicted defendants for forced labor.

- Name case is analogous because it also involves traffickers who smuggled the aliens into the United States and then used force and coercion to force the aliens into involuntary servitude.

- The fact that these cases started out as smuggling cases did not prevent a finding of trafficking and/or forced labor.

## 7. Name **is physically present in the United States as a result of trafficking:**

Name was brought to the United States by a human trafficker. The details are outlined in Name's declaration. Name entered the United States as a victim of trafficking because the coyote-trafficker fraudulently transported him/her to the United States for the purpose of working. The coyote-trafficker transported him/her to the United States and provided Name to the traffickers inside the United States, who then forced him/her to provide domestic labor for several weeks. Once Name became involved in the scheme, s/he did not feel that s/he could escape it until the traffickers ultimately released him/her.

Name is physically present in the United States on account of the trafficking. The T visa regulations at 8 C.F.R. § 214.11(g)(1) state the following:

"The physical presence requirement requires USCIS to consider the alien's presence in the United States at the time of application. The requirement reaches an alien who:

(i) Is present because he or she is currently being subjected to a severe form of trafficking in persons;

(ii) Was liberated from a severe form of trafficking in persons by an LEA;

(iii) Escaped a severe form of trafficking in persons before an LEA was involved, subject to paragraph (g)(2) of this section;

(iv) Was subject to a severe form of trafficking in persons at some point in the past and whose continuing presence in the United States is directly related to the original trafficking in persons; or

(v) Is present on account of the alien having been allowed entry into the United States for

> participation in investigative or judicial processes associated with an act or perpetrator of trafficking."

Name satisfies one or more of requirements listed in 8 C.F.R. § 214.11(g)(1) and therefore establishes that s/he is physically present in the United States on account of the trafficking. 8 C.F.R.§ 214.11(g)(1)(iii) provides that an applicant is physically present in the United States on account of the trafficking if he "[e]scaped a severe form of trafficking in persons before an LEA was involved, subject to paragraph (g)(2) of this section." This provision perfectly describes Name's situation. s/he escaped the traffickers/trafficking situation before the involvement of any law enforcement agency. The provision does not say "*recently* escaped" nor does it provide any limitation on *when* the escape must have occurred relative to the filing of the T visa application. The regulations make no mention of any particular time limit after which a person is no longer considered to be in the United States on account of the trafficking. In fact, USCIS has approved many T visa cases where the trafficking event took place many years before the applicant filed Form I-914. The only limitation is subsection (g)(2), which relates to a departure from the

United States after the act of trafficking. Because Name never left the United States after escaping from the trafficking situation, subsection (g)(2) does not apply to the application or limit the ability to establish physical presence.

In addition, the language in the Federal Register associated with the new regulations also explains that DHS expanded eligibility under the physical presence requirement in several different ways. One way is that DHS amended the regulation relating to an "opportunity to depart." A provision in the previous regulations titled "Opportunity to depart" provided that "[i]f the alien has escaped the traffickers before law enforcement became involved in the matter, he or she must show that he or she did not have a clear chance to leave the United States in the interim." The new regulations remove this regulatory 'opportunity to depart' requirement, however. The removal of that requirement "[p]rovides a qualitative benefit by removing an additional evidentiary burden for those victims of trafficking who escaped prior to LEA involvement," which indicates a desire to expand T visa eligibility. Because the regulations no longer require an applicant to prove he had an opportunity to depart, the length of time between the escape from the trafficking and the filing of the application is not relevant. Therefore, because Name's situation meets the clearly stated requirements of 8 C.F.R. § 214.11(g)(1)(iii), s/he is physically present in the United States on account of the trafficking.

Alternatively, Name also meets the requirements of 8 C.F.R. § 214.11(g)(1)(iv). That subsection provides that an applicant is physically present in the United States on account of the trafficking if he "[w]as subject to a severe form of trafficking in persons at some point in the past and whose continuing presence in the United States is directly related to the original trafficking in persons." This subsection again contemplates that an applicant can be physically present in the United States despite the trafficking occurring at some point in the past.

The regulations do not discuss what "directly related to the original trafficking" means, so we must conclude that it refers to a standard cause-and-effect type relationship. Name was brought into the United States by the coyote-trafficker. The last entry into the United States was the result of the victimization by the traffickers. After s/he escaped from the trafficking, s/he was fearful and traumatized. s/he tried to move forward with His/her life, while leaving the past behind the best Name could. Because Name's current presence in the United States resulted from events that directly stemmed from the trafficking, Name's continuing presence in the United States is directly related to the original trafficking.

**3.** Name **is willing to report the trafficking and comply with reasonable requests for assistance in the investigation and prosecution of acts of trafficking in persons:**

Despite Name fears, s/he remains willing to assist in the investigation of the trafficker in order to ensure that no other persons are tricked into coming to the U.S. through false promises and then trapped with no means to return home.

**4.** Name **would suffer extreme hardship involving severe and unusual harm upon removal to** Country:

Name is extremely vulnerable to being subjected to trafficking in persons again. Unemployment, underemployment and poverty are severe problems in Country.

Additionally, as the case is investigated, Name needs to stay in the United States to assist in the investigation of the trafficking violation committed by the trafficker. If Name leaves, the investigators will not have the benefit of His/her cooperation. Name intends to remain available as a witness and to assist in the investigation of this case.

**5.** Name **is deserving of discretion for the T Visa and waiver**

Name has the "usual" immigration violations of illegal entry to the United States, unlawful presence, unlawful employment, and working with false documents. However, Name has paid His/her taxes every single year, which is a presumptive good moral character factor. S/he strives to be contributing member of society.

For the reasons listed above and those that may be found within this application, we respectfully request that Name be granted a T-Visa.

Sincerely,

Attorney

# APPENDIX H:

---

## T Visa Index of Documents

## INDEX OF DOCUMENTS

### APPLICANT, NAME

- ❖ Form I-912, Fee Waiver Request

- ❖ Fee Waiver Request Affidavit and supporting documentation (Taxes, W-2s, paystubs, proof of expenses and dependents)

- ❖ Form G-28;

- ❖ Form I-914;

- ❖ Form I-192;

- ❖ Two passport-style photos;

❖ Copy of Applicant's Birth Certificate with Certified Translation

❖ Copy of applicant's passport identification page

## SUPPORTING DOCUMENTS TO I-914

A. Evidence demonstrating that applicant is victim of trafficking and physical presence on account of trafficking:

   1. Declaration;

      i. Declaration of applicant in support of I-914 and I-192.

   2. Human Trafficking Indicators worksheet;

B. Documents in Support of Cooperation and Assistance in Investigation:

   1. Click here to enter text.

[Example: Copy of email to DOL reporting trafficking on ____ date; and copy of email to DOL following up and asking for an interview and/or T visa certification to be provided as a result of the survivor having reported the trafficking to DOL]

## SUPPORTING DOCUMENTS TO I-192 FOR PRINCIPAL AND DERIVATIVE APPLICANTS

A. Declaration of derivative in support of I-192.

B. Certified criminal record for the applicant (if applicable)

C. Good moral character support letters explaining why the criminal activity by the applicant should be forgiven in light of its connection to the trafficking or in light of the applicant having rehabilitated (optional)

# APPENDIX I:

---

**T Visa Approval Letter**

Click or tap to enter a date.

<u>DELIVERY:</u> Choose an item.

Click or tap here to enter text.

Click or tap here to enter text.

Click or tap here to enter text.

**RE: Important Information - T Visa Approval**

Dear Click or tap here to enter text.:

We are pleased to advise you that your T visa application has been approved. Enclosed is the original T-visa approval notice, which has an "I-94 card" attached and is valid from Click or tap here to enter text. to Click or tap here to enter text. Our representation of you on this matter has ended now that your visa is approved, but we ask that you read this letter carefully and keep in touch with us in the future.

**Keep your T visa I-94 card safe**

The I-94 card and T visa approval notice are very important – the I-94 card is your proof that you are in America in lawful status. Now that you have a Click or tap here to enter text. passport, you should staple the I-94 card into the passport and keep these documents safe. All T visa recipients are required to maintain a current passport. If your T visa approval/I-94 card or EAD are lost or stolen, you must obtain a replacement. Federal law requires that you keep your I-94 card with you at all times.

**EAD work permit**

By now, you should also have received your EAD work permit, which is valid from Click or tap here to enter text. to Click or tap here to enter text. The EAD ("Employment Authorization Document") is valid proof of work authorization and allows you to work for any employer in the United States. You may use the EAD work permit to apply for or replace a Social Security Card. You can also use it to obtain a driver's license or ID card. When you apply for jobs, you are allowed to say you are "work authorized." Remember, though, you are not a permanent resident or US citizen yet, so you have to be careful to fill out any I-9 forms for new jobs correctly. Be sure to contact us if you have questions.

## Please send us a copy of EAD; mark your Calendar for important dates; and save money for the future!

1. If you have not done so already, please send us a copy of your EAD work permit so that we may keep a copy on file for you.

2. Please set a reminder on your calendar to get in touch with us to begin your green card process in the future. As you may remember, the T visa is valid for four (4) years, but you have 2 options now:

    a. Make an appointment and pay for a consultation to talk about the possibility of applying for Permanent Residency ("Early Adjustment of Status") due to your T-1 investigation being closed with the FBI and/or another agency; or

b. To apply for lawful permanent residency (i.e. the green card). Because it takes several months to get ready to apply for Adjustment of Status to Permanent Resident, we will want to discuss your permanent residency eligibility well in advance of your 3-year T-visa anniversary. Many clients visit us once a year to go over the requirements for permanent residency, to make sure they will qualify in the future and to discuss any new changes in the immigration laws, etc. We would be happy to meet with you if you choose to do so.

3. Remember, you will also need to save money for the permanent residency application process. Government fees increase about 20% every two years, and of course there will be legal fees and other costs associated with obtaining your green card.

## Change of Address: Form AR-11

All non-U.S. citizens, including non-immigrant T-visa holders, must notify USCIS within ten (10) days of moving to a new residence. Remember, just updating the post office of a new address is not enough! You must file an AR-11 even for a temporary change of address. To notify USCIS, you can fill out and file the change of address form (AR-11) at www.uscis.gov. Failure to follow this rule may subject you to deportation or criminal prosecution. The USCIS website contains the proper AR-11 Change of Address form, mailing address and instructions; or for a fee our office can handle this for you. Also keep a complete copy for your records. You can also send us a copy for our file on you, if you wish.

## Effect of Criminal Activity or Future Immigration Violations

The Immigration Service was very forgiving when they granted your T-visa application. Please understand that if you break any laws in the future, the Immigration Service does not have to forgive you again.

Even the most basic criminal offense may affect your immigration status, even if the immigration authorities are not notified by the police immediately. If you are charged with a crime, let us know immediately so that we can advise you on the possible immigration consequences. We expect that you will notify us immediately of any criminal charge (i.e. the same day if possible!)

I especially want to point out that drunk driving, drugs, and domestic violence are major offenses for people who only have a temporary immigration status, such as the T-visa. It is very important that you keep your criminal record clean over the next 3 to 4 years. If you don't, you could lose your T-visa status, be deported, and/or be denied a green card in the future.

## International Travel

Your Employment Authorization Card and T-visa I-94 are **NOT** travel documents. I know the term "T-visa" sounds like you are approved to travel in and out of the United States, but the T-visa that you have is only valid for being "inside the United States." It does not give you permission to travel in and out of the United States.

If you leave the United States, you will be required to apply for a separate T-visa with the U.S. Consulate overseas to re-enter the United States. However, there may be issues that prevent you from being granted the T-visa in order to return to the United States. In fact, any waivers granted (for illegal entry or illegal work, for example), would have to be applied for all over again with the consulate, and there is no guarantee that if you leave America, you will be approved to return. If you need to travel outside the United States, please contact us before making plans to leave the United States.

## Prior removal orders

If you were in deportation previously, we may need to file a motion to terminate this status. Prior deportation history also makes it harder to obtain a visa abroad. Please contact us to discuss this matter if you have had any deportation history so that we can review your specific needs again.

## Applying for visas for family members

If you are interested in legalizing your family members or applying for a visa for a family member, please contact us now so that we can review the individual case. A consultation fee typically applies for each new individual consultation; you can call our office to discuss scheduling an appointment to discuss family members' cases.

If you have children or step-children who need a lawful immigration status, please contact us immediately, since there are age-limits (and other types of limits) on which children and step-children can legalize.

## Taxation

You are required to pay U.S. taxes on all your income. Your failure to file and pay taxes may result in negative consequences if you later apply for permanent resident status or US citizenship. I recommend that you have a professional certified public accountant ("CPA") assist with the filing of your taxes each year so that you correctly report your income to the U.S. government. Working under the table or "for cash," and failing to disclose that earned income on a tax return, can have serious consequences (penalties, fines, visa revocation, etc.). Please be sure that you correctly file your taxes. Our office cannot provide tax advice but can refer you to an accountant if you need help.

## Social Security

You can now file an application for a Social Security Card by presenting your T-visa approval and EAD work permit. You should contact the Social Security Administration to apply for a new Social Security Card. If you previously used an ITIN, you can ask that your earnings under the ITIN be credited toward your Social Security Account (so that you can get a larger pension in the future). If you previously had a valid SSN, you still need to go in-person (again) to the Social Security Administration so that they can update your Social Security Records. If you have problems with SSA, please contact us.

## Driver's license

After you apply for your Social Security Card, you should be able to apply for a driver's license or identification card. I strongly recommend that you obtain a state-issued identification or driver's license. If you have problems with DMV, please contact us.

## Military Duty

If you are a man ages 18 through 25 and living in the U.S., then you must register with Selective Service. According to law, a man must register with Selective

Service within 30 days of his 18th birthday. Selective Service will accept late registrations but not after a man has reached age 26. You may be denied benefits or a job if you have not registered. You can register at any U.S. Post Office and do not need a social security number to register with the Selective Service. **When you do obtain a social security number, let Selective Service know**. You can visit the Selective Service website for more information at: www.sss.gov . For example, the SSS website currently says, "Noncitizens who are not required to register with Selective Service include men who are in the U.S. on student or visitor visas, and men who are part of a diplomatic or trade mission and their families. Almost all other male noncitizens are required to register, including illegal aliens, legal permanent residents, and refugees. The general rule is that if a male noncitizen takes up residency in the U.S. before his 26th birthday, he must register with Selective Service."

## General info on Adjustment of Status for T-visa holders (i.e., the green card)

Applicants for adjustment of status holding a "T" visa must have been lawfully admitted to the United States as a "T" nonimmigrant and must continue to hold such status at the time of application. In addition, "T" visa holders demonstrate:

(1) Continuous Physical presence in the United States for a continuous period of at least three years since the date of admission as a "T" nonimmigrant; and

(2) No unreasonable refusal to provide assistance in the criminal investigation or prosecution; and

(3) Be eligible for a discretionary grant of Adjustment of Status.

Evidence of continuous physical presence is required; this can be provided by college transcripts, employment records, or installment payments (e.g., monthly rent receipts, utility bills, etc.) during the requisite time period. So, you may want to save these documents over the next few years. You should also save evidence of any facts that might merit a favorable exercise of discretion, such as letters of good moral character, membership in community associations, awards, prizes, and anything else showing that you have been living in the US as a good person. Learning more English, improving your education, and generally being a productive member of society will help you with your future green card application. It will also help you in the future if you wish to apply for US citizenship. We also recommend that you be a good record-keeper, meaning that you save copies of medical bills, medical records, and anything that might further demonstrate you would experience hardship if not allowed to reside in the US. Such items have been very helpful in a variety of immigration cases, so being organized and keeping records is a good idea.

## Jury duty; Voting

You are <u>not</u> eligible to vote in America and you are <u>not</u> eligible for jury duty. Only American citizens can vote and participate in jury duty. Sometimes the DMV or voter registration advocates accidentally sign up immigrants to vote, and it causes problems. So, if this happens to you by mistake, please contact us immediately.

## Conclusion

As you can see, having T-visa status is helpful, but it is just the beginning of your immigration process. It is very important that you seek out proper legal advice regarding maintaining your T-visa status and preparing for permanent residency in the future. The U.S. Government has given you a wonderful opportunity to remain legally in the US, and you will need to work hard to preserve lawful status.

Our office tries to update former clients of new developments in the law. However, the law changes constantly. You are responsible for contacting us with questions and/or retaining us for future legal services.

Sincerely,


<u>Attorney</u>

# APPENDIX J:

---

**Letter to DOJ requesting confirmation that the investigation is closed**

**To:** 'T-Adjustment.Cert@usdoj.gov' <T-Adjustment.Cert@usdoj.gov>

**Cc:** 'Hilary.Axam@usdoj.gov' <Hilary.Axam@usdoj.gov>

To Whom It May Concern,

Mr. _____'s T Visa case was approved. Thank you for allowing him to report the trafficking to the DOJ Human Trafficking Prosecution Unit.

I just wanted to confirm with you that the DOJ's investigation is done. If you could just email me back to confirm that I would appreciate it. You do not need to sign any T certification.

**Name:**

**Gender:**

**Date of T Visa Approval:**

**Date of Trafficking:**

**Location of Trafficking:**

**Reported to:**

**Interview Status:**

**Other Notes:** we believe there was no further investigation due to [give reason]. T visa approval notice attached.

Sincerely,

Attorney

# ACKNOWLEDGMENTS

**Alexandra would like to acknowledge the following people:**

- My husband, Manuel Lozano, who is a true partner in every sense of the word. Thank you for encouraging me to jump right in to the T Visa and figure out how to make it work for our clients. Thank you for your support as I have written this book. I have written during family time, soccer practices, and during late nights while you have been trying to sleep, and all you have ever said is, "That's so awesome! You're doing great work." You make every single thing in this life possible. I love you with all my heart and soul.

- My *preciosas* Khloe and Isabella. Thank you for looking over my shoulder with excitement and asking, "Is your new book done yet?" and always asking me about it. Your pure hearts and endless love make me believe that a better world exists.

- Magaly who is wise beyond her years. I know that I have shared stories with you that are more than most teenagers would ever hear about, but I know that you will carry them with you and transform the world. I cherish our conversations and time together.

- Noelia who is a fiercely independent young woman who challenges me to the deepest parts of myself and teaches me how I can be better. You are a gift.

- My little boy, Quique, who never runs out of kisses and hugs for mami. I hope you will grow into a man who uses his voice for women.

- Bridgette Bennett who first told me about smuggling turned trafficking during my Amiga Business Bootcamp in Miami. She connected me with Helen and the rest is history.

- Stephanie Morales who has helped me build my smuggling turned trafficking arguments and who has taught me through example and her very hard work how to improve my T Visa case preparation.

- Amy Rios who learned how to write T Visa declarations and T Visa legal arguments on the spot and who is a huge drive in the reason for our continuing success with T Visas. You rise to every challenge and new idea. Thank you for everything.

- My Amigas who have shared ideas, legal theories, and supported one another as we have all collectively learned this very important body of law. You are my eternal lifeline. We are in this together and there is no way I could do this work without you.

- Helen Tarokic a woman for whom there are no words. You inspire. You transform. You are one in a million. I am honored to have authored this book together.

# ACKNOWLEDGMENTS

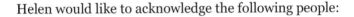

Helen would like to acknowledge the following people:

- Ante Tarokic, my amazing Croatian-American husband, who was so impressed and supportive when I said I was going to publish a book. Ante makes me laugh every day. When I come home after listening to horrific stories of human trafficking, he finds a way to make me feel happy, loved, and safe.

- Adriana, my kind, smart, 6-year-old daughter, and my 2-year-old son, Ante, who surprises me every day with his new words and way of looking at the world. Adriana has already had her first HBO appearance as a toddler on the John Oliver show Last Week Tonight, on an episode about the immigration courts (https://www.youtube.com/watch?v=9fB0GBwJ2 QA). Our children get to see what I do for a living in small doses and have helped me be a better advocate.

- My mother, Koraljka Jugovic, who has encouraged me to be a strong, independent, community-driven woman. My mom is the better version of me and is the best grandma to our kids. As I write this, she has been teaching my children how to pick olives and make olive oil on the islands of Dalmatia.

- My father, Valentin Jugovic, who survived various workplace and government abuses, involuntary servitude, and domestic violence situations as a child and young adult. He somehow managed to break that cycle and be a kind, loving father despite a lack of resources. My father and mother immigrated from Yugoslavia to the US in the 1960s with the hope of a better life for us all.

- Emma Buckthal, a supervising attorney at the Erie County Bar Association Volunteer Lawyers Project, Inc. Emma taught me how to do my first T visa and has flown around the US with me to teach others how to do them. When we're done teaching human trafficking lessons, we look at photos of fuzzy animals and funny GIFs to get back to "normal." Emma is just one of many lawyers who helped me improve our technique.

- Margaret Taylor, my immigration law professor at Wake Forest Law, who has been a friend and mentor from the beginning. Professor Taylor has inspired generations of lawyers to pursue a career in immigration law, and she continues to inspire me on a daily basis. My friend, I cannot imagine life without you.

- My previous supervising attorneys: Paul Zulkie, Gerry Chapman, Pamela Mick, Susan McLean, and Jeremy McKinney, who taught me much of what I know today about immigration law.

- Our entire AILA Carolinas Chapter, the AIC and AILA National, for teaching me and helping me teach.

- Anna Lane Barfield, Katherine Haddock, Pam Mansbery, Luz Naranjo, Heather Ziemba, and the rest of our amazing team at Helen Tarokic Law PLLC.